Claiming the Beatitudes

Claiming the Beatitudes

Nine Stories from a New Generation

Anne Sutherland Howard

THE
ALBAN
INSTITUTE

Herndon, Virginia
www.alban.org

The Alban Institute
2121 Cooperative Way, Suite 100
Herndon, VA 20171-5370

Unless otherwise noted, all Scripture quotations are from the New Revised Standard Version of the Bible, copyright © 1989, Division of Christian Education of the National Council of the Churches of Christ in the United States of America, and are used by permission.

Scripture quotations marked RSV are from the Revised Standard Version of the Bible, copyright © 1952 [2nd edition, 1971] by the Division of Christian Education of the National Council of the Churches of Christ in the United States of America. Used by permission. All rights reserved.

Cover design by Tobias Becker, Bird Box Design.

Cover art: The Best Supper © Jan L. Richardson (janrichardson.com)

Library of Congress Cataloging-in-Publication Data

Library of Congress Cataloging-in-Publication Data

Howard, Anne Sutherland.
    Claiming the Beatitudes : nine stories from a new generation / Anne Sutherland Howard.
        p. cm.
    Includes bibliographical references.
    ISBN 978-1-56699-384-5
    1. Beatitudes. 2. Christian youth—Religious life—United States.
I. Title.

    BT382.H68 2009
    241.5'3—dc22
                                        2008051510

        10   11   12   13   14   VP   6   5   4   3   2

THE BEATITUDES

Matthew 5:1–12

When Jesus saw the crowds, he went up the mountain; and after he sat down, his disciples came to him. Then he began to speak, and taught them, saying:

"Blessed are the poor in spirit, for theirs is the kingdom of heaven.

"Blessed are those who mourn, for they will be comforted.

"Blessed are the meek, for they will inherit the earth.

"Blessed are those who hunger and thirst for justice, for they will be satisfied.

"Blessed are the merciful, for they will receive mercy.

"Blessed are the pure in heart, for they will see God.

"Blessed are the peacemakers, for they will be called children of God.

"Blessed are those who are persecuted for justice's sake, for theirs is the kingdom of heaven.

"Blessed are you when people revile you and persecute you and utter all kinds of evil against you falsely on my account. Rejoice and be glad, for your reward is great in heaven, for in the same way they persecuted the prophets who were before you."[1]

CONTENTS

june 27

july 11

july 25

FOREWORD

Reading this book reminded me of Augustine's exultant praise of God some sixteen centuries ago. He addressed God as, "O Beauty so ancient and so fresh!" This book is about the other two parts of the triad of beauty, truth and goodness. It is about truth and goodness, so ancient and so fresh. And, in its own way, it is also about beauty.

Its ancient subject matter is one of the most famous parts of the teaching of Jesus, the beatitudes that begin the Sermon on the Mount in Matthew's Gospel. These familiar sayings pronounce blessing on the poor, the mourners, the meek, the seekers of justice, the compassionate, the pure in heart, the peacemakers, and the persecuted. They are challenging sayings—in the first century and now.

The freshness of this book lies in its twenty-first-century voices—in it we hear stories from the lives of nine members of The Beatitudes Society, an organization conceived in 2004 and born in 2005. Its purpose is raising consciousness among seminarians about the kind of life envisioned by the beatitudes—a life of compassion, justice, and peace, grounded in God as disclosed by Jesus. The Society has more than four hundred members in chapters in twenty seminaries and continues to grow.

The nine chapters that form this book's heart all begin with an interview with one of the members of the Society about what a particular beatitude has come to mean to them. Their stories are marked by discovery and insight, passion and conviction.

All but one of the nine are twenty-somethings and thirty-somethings, the generation that many older Christians long to see more involved in the life of the church. As I lecture in church settings around the country, I am often asked, "Where are they? How do we attract them?" Important questions.

In this book you will meet a number of them. You will not learn strategies for attracting more of them—that is not what the book is about. But you will be encouraged by their presence in the church and their passion for Jesus. And you are likely to learn from them.

We also hear another twenty-first-century voice, the author's. Anne Sutherland Howard is an Episcopal priest and Executive Director of The Beatitudes Society. In each chapter, she offers her own reflections about the interview and about the particular beatitude. She skillfully and gracefully integrates scholarly understandings and voices with her own insights to suggest meanings and applications of the beatitudes for our own time. This is a rich book—not only informative, but inspirational in the best sense of that word: it can move you and change you.

To return to the beatitudes themselves, they occupy a place of particular importance in Matthew's Gospel. They are the first words of Jesus' "inaugural address," the Sermon on the Mount in Matthew 5–7.

Prior to Matthew 5, Matthew narrates the stories of Jesus' birth, his baptism by John, his temptations in the wilderness, his call of the first disciples, and the beginning of his public activity, emphasizing his role as a healer. But in all of Matthew's first four chapters, we are given only one line of Jesus' public teaching. "Repent, for the kingdom of heaven has come near" (4:17).

It is an important line. Matthew crystallizes the message of Jesus in his first public words as the coming of "the kingdom" and the invitation and imperative to "repent" (whose Greek roots mean "to go beyond the mind that you have"). Mark, our earliest Gospel, written a decade or two before Matthew, also reports that that the first words of Jesus' public activity were about the coming of the kingdom: "The kingdom of God has come near—repent" (Mark 1:15). Think of the coming of God's kingdom as the message of Jesus reduced to a bumper-sticker slogan.

Importantly, "heaven" in Matthew's phrase "kingdom of heaven" does not refer to the afterlife, as the word most commonly suggests in English. Rather, as Anne Howard points out in this book, "the kingdom of *heaven*" is Matthew's phrase for what Jesus in Mark and Luke speaks of as "the kingdom of *God*." Matthew changes the phrase "kingdom of *God*" to "kingdom of *heaven*" not because he's thinking of life after death, but because of his Jewish reverence for "God," which meant avoiding saying the word by substituting synonyms.

Thus, and also importantly, the kingdom of heaven, the kingdom of God, is not about the next world, but life in this world. Matthew himself makes this clear in his version of the Lord's Prayer (6:9–13), which is also in the Sermon on the Mount: "Your kingdom come, your will be done, *on earth* as it is in heaven" (6.10).

As the contemporary New Testament scholar John Dominic Crossan says: according to Jesus, heaven's in great shape—earth is where the problems are. God's kingdom is *for the earth*. Heaven's kingdom, God's kingdom, is about *this* world. It is about what life would be like *on earth* if God were king and the rulers of this world were not, if God were lord *on earth* and the lords of this world were not.

This—the meaning of God's kingdom on earth—is what Matthew expands in the Sermon on the Mount, beginning with the beatitudes. They are the opening words of the inaugural address of the kingdom of God.

We do not know if Jesus spoke the beatitudes one after the other as Matthew reports, and at the beginning of a three-chapter long Sermon on the Mount. In fact, it seems unlikely. The Gospel of Luke has four of the beatitudes, fewer than half of Matthew's, and in a different order and slightly different form (Luke 6:20–23). Moreover, Jesus as an itinerant and oral teacher would have said his sayings (and told his parables) many times. One cannot imagine an itinerant oral teacher using these remarkable sayings (and stories) only once.

Thus the beatitudes (and the Sermon on the Mount as a whole) are best seen as Matthew's perception (and collection) of what was most central to Jesus and the kingdom he proclaimed. Think of the beatitudes and the Sermon on the Mount as a house made of bricks: Jesus supplied the bricks, the individual sayings; Matthew put them together into a construction.

So perhaps we should think of the beatitudes as individual sayings of Jesus. Perhaps we should imagine them as one-liners, left hanging in the air. Or perhaps we should think of them as one-sentence summations of oral teachings expounded at greater length, as "texts" for a discourse, perhaps for the sake of dialogue, debate, discussion. It is easy to imagine. Jesus says, "Blessed are the poor." To which the response might be, "Blessed are the poor??? What one earth do you mean?" Jesus may well have practiced participatory pedagogy. It would be consistent with what else we know about him.

In this book, the beatitudes are treated separately, one in each chapter. This is as it should be. Of course they are related to each other. But each warrants—indeed, requires—the kind of reflection that we do not have time for when we hear them read as a collection. We find ourselves saying, "Wait, wait—Jesus, I need time to reflect on the first one, and you're already saying the second and the third and the fourth. Slow down!" This book provides time and words and insights and suggestions for this reflection.

Finally, given their location at the beginning of Matthew's first exposition of what the coming of God's kingdom means, the beatitudes speak of God's passion and the passion of Jesus. God's passion—what God is passionate about – is, according to the Bible, *this* world. There is no denial of an afterlife in this recognition. But God's love, God's passion, is *this* world—the created world, the world of nature and human beings and all creatures. This claim is grounded in the story of creation in the first chapter of Genesis: after each day of creation, God pronounces it "good" and at the climax, "very good."

It is also grounded in the best-known verse in the New Testament, John 3:16, which begins, "For God so loved *the world*." Not just me, not just you and me, not just Christians, not just human beings, but "the world." This is God's passion.

And Jesus is for Christians the decisive revelation of God—of what can be seen of God in a human life. What can be seen of God in a human life is not God's omnipotence or omniscience—a human being who was all-powerful and all-knowing would not be one of us. Rather, what can be seen of God in a human life is God's character and passion—what God is like, and what God is passionate about. This is what we see in Jesus and his message—and for Matthew and his community, that begins with the beatitudes.

And so, to Anne Howard and the members and supporters of The Beatitudes Society, I am grateful—for this book and for what they are seeking to do. "Blessed are those who hunger and thirst for justice, for they will be filled; and blessed are the peacemakers, for they will be called children of God." None of this is about rewards—it is about God's passion, and the passion of Jesus, for life in this world. This is what we are invited to—this is the path of blessing.

Marcus J. Borg

Parables from a new generation

I have a hunch this book began the day the World Book encyclopedia set arrived at our house in Red Wing, Minnesota. In anticipation of the big day, my dad had built a special bookcase and placed it in our front hall, right under the picture of Jesus (yes, the same one that hung in the church basement Sunday School room, that one with the soft brown eyes and the wavy brown hair). We all gathered to open the big cardboard box, and took turns—my mother and father and brothers and I—taking out a "letter" at a time and placing it in the new bookcase. The books were red and blue leatherette, stamped with gold, and filled with treasure.

On winter mornings, one of my favorite things was to get up before everybody else, take a "letter"—I liked F with all the Flags and S because it was so big—and sit behind the big chair in the living room corner, my toes warming on the furnace vent, reading entry after entry, definition after definition. I just loved to "look it up."

I came to love definitions. But I have learned in the course of the intervening years that a love of definitions is not such a good thing for a pastor: very few things in the life of faith can be neatly defined. Despite learning Luther's Small Catechism in my Lutheran Sunday School, I grew up to become a questioning Episcopal priest. Faith, I would argue, and all things theological, cannot be defined by any precise catechism, but must always be illustrated by experience and narrative. It's our questions and doubts, not crisp answers or absolute certainty, that lead us into lively faith.

But still, it's comforting to have a list of definitions, a dictionary or encyclopedia to say that this-means-this and that-means-that or, even better, this-illustrates-that.

I come to the beatitudes in Matthew's gospel with something of my little-girl curiosity about definitions (what do the beatitudes mean?) along with a lifetime of adult experience that tells me that we learn and live our theology through our individual and collective narrative. The rich treasury of stories that we inherit as Christians describes how God acts in our world and in our lives.

So I have gathered here stories of nine contemporary young people who are trying to live lives of faith, trying to make some connections between their faith tradition and the world's concerns, young people who ask: "What would the beatitudes look like today? Is it possible to live a beatitudes life in today's world?"

I have heard these questions in my work with The Beatitudes Society[1] as I've traveled back and forth across the country, talking with students about their passion for justice, hearing their questions and concerns about the intersection of faith and public life. I hear comments like these:

"I just preached about the need for a single-payer national health plan, but a group of small business owners in my church have come forward to complain about politics in the pulpit. Now what do I do?"

"We tried to start a campaign to 'green' our seminary, but we couldn't get enough support from our classmates.

They said, 'we're here to study theology—why do we have to bother about the environment?'"

"A group of us students are planning a campus forum about same-sex marriage, but we've been told that the trustees won't let this happen. How can we get folks talking?"

"Some people in my bible study group at my wealthy suburban parish say that the first beatitude is about spiritual poverty. Is that what Jesus meant by 'Blessed are the poor in spirit?'"

And I also hear another type of question: "We're just worn out on my campus, running from one protest to another, one march to another, one conference to another, one project to another. How do we keep it all going?" or "It's hard to keep the juices flowing when we work so hard and nothing changes—what sustains you in the long haul for justice work?" "There are too many issues, where do we start?"

As I've listened to their questions, I hear my own echo back at me. I also hear the same kinds of concerns I've heard over the last twenty-plus years as a preacher, the questions of those who come through the church doors wondering if the church or the bible has anything to say about the recent shooting on yet another campus or the boarded up foreclosed houses dotting the neighborhood or the cutbacks in the county school budget or their granddaughter's revolving door relationship with the local drug rehab center.

I believe the students and their questions can give all of us some new insights for our own questions, as we all struggle to connect the dots between our faith and our actions. I believe they can help us "live the beatitudes" in our world. I know they help me, and I'd like to share what I'm learning from them. I count these students as cherished fellow learners as we explore together the meaning of the words of Jesus we now call the Sermon on the Mount.

I am not an expert on Matthew, but instead a committed student of the biblical narrative who seeks out the wisdom of others in my quest to interpret both ancient scripture and the stories and issues of our day. I go to these teachers with the same eagerness and even more questions than I had when I went to the World Book of my childhood. My understanding of the beatitudes has been influenced by three scholars in particular: I am grateful for the insights as well as the generous personal consultation offered to me by Marcus Borg, Frederick Borsch, and Glen Stassen. Marcus Borg's work has reintroduced me to Jesus as one filled with passion for God's kingdom, a kingdom very much at hand in our world. For nearly thirty years, my reading, teaching, and preaching the story of Jesus have been enlightened by Fred Borsch's work on the polyvalent meaning of the parables. Glen Stassen, ethicist at Fuller Theological Seminary, has influenced how I understand the grace-filled ethics of the beatitudes. All three have deepened my understanding of Jesus as a wisdom teacher rooted in the tradition of the Hebrew prophets and very much concerned with the harsh realities of daily life in first-century Palestine.

The beatitudes are spiritual practices leading us, as Matthew suggests, to be the "salt of the earth" and the "light of the world," but I have learned that they lead us not as a demanding moral code or a set of impossible ideals to achieve, but rather as a way to recognize God present and active in our world today. Far from being an ethics of idealism, the beatitudes point to the realities of our world and the reality of God's healing and reconciling love. "Idealism speaks to people who are not what the ideals urge. It promises that if they live by the ideals they will get rewards. . . . The beatitudes are not like that," Stassen says. "They are based not on the perfection of the disciples but on the coming of God's grace, already experienced in Jesus."[2]

If we interpret the beatitudes as a set of rules to live by we sever them from their roots in the tradition of the Jewish prophets. Matthew's community was steeped in Isaiah, and Jesus quotes Isaiah more than any other prophet. Isaiah announced again and again the signs of God's presence in the world, using language about peace and light and justice and healing and liberation and joy. Each one of the beatitudes echoes Isaiah's description of the reign of God.

These brief sayings give us a lens through which to see Jesus and the God he proclaimed. Through these words, and through his alternative way in the world, Jesus points to a God who is always doing something new, a God who engages this world with healing mercy, endless compassion, and liberating justice. We see a God who is most concerned about those who have the least. The beatitudes give us not only a way to see God, but a way to see our world, and they give us something concrete to do about what we see, as they call us to participate in God's kingdom. As St. Augustine said, (and Marcus Borg quotes): "God without us will not; and we without God cannot."[3]

The emerging leaders whose stories follow know this; they claim the beatitudes of Jesus not as a description of a future heavenly realm, but as a prescription for vital discipleship now. With them, I believe that the beatitudes were offered to the early church as both encouraging comfort and as a stirring manifesto for a way of life that ran radically counter to the prevailing ethos of the Roman Empire. These words of blessing are as defiant as Mary's Magnificat and as bold as Jesus' first sermon at Nazareth. The beatitudes had the power to change lives in the first century, and they hold that same power today, shaping a new generation of leaders and giving them a word of daring hope to bring to the communities they will serve.

I hope to illustrate that daring hope, presenting these stories as new parables for practicing the life-giving values expressed in the beatitudes. Each chapter looks at one beatitude and one person's way to "live" that blessing in their daily life; their story is followed by my reflection which often includes a look at other teachings of Jesus that illustrate the beatitude. Because I am convinced that the biblical story is meant to be read and reflected upon in community—the text comes alive when spoken aloud and our own stories rub up against the stories of our ancestors—I have ended each chapter with a few reflection questions for individuals and small groups who want to continue the conversation about living the beatitudes today.

I have been privileged to hear the stories of these leaders who claim the beatitudes, and I want to introduce them to you. Their stories are as varied as the tellers themselves. Some speak in careful and articulate paragraphs, some muse off-the-cuff. They come from different denominations and different schools, from Boston to Berkeley and many places in between. Some are students, some have recently graduated from divinity school and are serving in churches and schools and organizations across the country. But all are committed to finding new ways to live the beatitudes in our day. I invite you to meet these emerging leaders and enter their stories in the hope that you will recognize something of your own journey in theirs.

A word of caution to the reader who's looking for a Top Ten Best kind of list: America's Most Likely Future Presidents, Popes, and Pulitzer Prize Winners. The people you will meet here are leaders, to be sure, and a few of these names may show up in headlines someday. But their stories are not impossible hero stories; these are simply people of commitment and conviction and courage who invite us to join them in their daily practice.

In chapter one, "Blessed are the poor in spirit," Chris Wendell offers "a third way" to see the relationship between poverty and wealth, and discovers the beloved community. This first chapter is a little longer than the others, as this first beatitude serves as a foundation for the ones that follow.

In chapter two, "Blessed are those who mourn," Stefani Schatz finds church in a pub, takes us through a Good Friday world into the joy of Easter, and shows us the practice of hospitality.

In chapter three, "Blessed are the meek," Alexander Carpenter pushes against American notions of maleness and patriarchy on behalf of the coming generations who will inherit this fragile earth of ours.

In chapter four, "Blessed are those who hunger and thirst for justice, Greta Leach responds to a deep desire for transformation and begins to build a bridge into the future.

In chapter five, "Blessed are the merciful," April Blaine looks in the mirror and discovers that it can be harder to receive than to give mercy.

In chapter six, "Blessed are the pure in heart," Mary Emily Duba and her many questions show us the face of God.

In chapter seven, "Blessed are the peacemakers," Kent Sensenig practices local and daily ways to make peace.

In chapter eight, "Blessed are those who are persecuted for justice's sake," Jeremy takes up the cause of "the persecuted of the persecuted" as he fights the new global slave trade.

In chapter nine, "Blessed are you persecuted," Obadiah Ballinger moves through persecution to rejoicing in his work for equal justice in Connecticut.

And in chapter ten, I offer a way for us to be "salty people" who can illumine the world and turn it upside down in the radical spirit of Jesus.

CHAPTER ONE

Blessed are the poor in spirit

"Blessed are the poor in spirit, for theirs
is the kingdom of heaven."—Matthew 5:3

CHRISTOPHER'S STORY

For Christopher Wendell, the first beatitude is about a
"third way." It's a third way of seeing poverty and wealth:
instead of ignoring the divisions that wealth and poverty
create or being paralyzed into inaction by them, we can
see how they unite us, not just divide us. This third way
of seeing means choosing a spirituality of abundance in
the face of a culture of scarcity. It's a way of seeing that
he learned as a child at his family's kitchen table.

"I lived in the same house in San Francisco from age
two until I left for college. It's still home base, right near
all the schools we went to, the park we played at," he
says. "We were a family of eight and we always cooked for
ten or twelve. We always had people over for dinner; our
kitchen table was an endless cycle of people, homework,
snacks, and meals. Everybody was welcome there."

A recent graduate of Episcopal Divinity School in
Cambridge, Massachusetts, Chris is now serving a suburban parish in Wellesley, Massachusetts. He admits it's
not the kind of church or community that might come to
mind when one hears "blessed are the poor in spirit." He
is keenly aware of the privileged community he serves.

"I work in a materially rich parish," he says. "While not everyone is financially stable, looking at it from a global perspective I serve a wealthy congregation in a wealthy community in a wealthy state in a wealthy country."

Living in a wealthy community in a wealthy state in a wealthy country is not unfamiliar to Chris. His childhood spanned the tech boom of the 1980s and 1990s in the San Francisco Bay Area, and his family was part of that boom. "San Francisco was in the middle of a whole lot of new wealth. My dad was a venture capitalist who worked in Palo Alto, helping to grow companies that could be transformative for the whole world; he had contact with cutting-edge technologies. We grew up learning that innovation could change the world and we could be participants in it. In that environment each of us felt like we could be a mover, we were responsible for change, for making things better."

"Making things better" has been Chris's priority through school and now in his parish ministry. He says that "making things better" in the global sense begins with the transformation of people: their souls, their minds, their hearts, and it is this that drew Chris towards parish ministry.

"The transforming Spirit of God comes not just through individuals deep in prayer, but to communities working for growth and change together," Chris says. "Parishes are unique communities of trust, places where people can begin to take risks of all kinds with each other. One kind of risk that the church invites us to take is to see a wider range of the economic spectrum—to open our eyes to how interconnected the financial realities of the well-off and the destitute really are. Parishes are places to come to Jesus, literally in the sharing of a simple meal, and figuratively in the sense of finding the strength to recognize that material wealth can create spiritual poverty."

Chris is quick to point out that he does not interpret "poor in spirit" or spiritual poverty as a spiritualization of the beatitude or any kind of attempt to sidestep the harsh realities of economic poverty. He sees spiritual poverty as an avenue for the materially rich to recognize their relationship to the materially poor—the third way.

"For people like me who have enough to eat, who live in stable circumstances, people who are materially rich, it can be hard to recognize the ways in which we are poor, the ways in which we still have unmet needs," he says. "The myth of affluence is that it's completely satisfying. But we are all poor in some ways, we are all poor in spirit—that's what the first beatitude is all about. When a person of social privilege can become aware of their spiritual poverty, of their distance from those who are materially poor, it gives him or her an experience of need, of incompleteness. This is the fundamental first step in creating the space for growth and for more just relationships."

One way in which Chris tries to reveal this need for relationship across class lines is by taking his church youth group to do Katrina rebuilding work at Mission on the Bay in Bay St. Louis, Mississippi. "Our congregation went down to the Gulf Coast the first summer after Katrina and saw the suffering and loss. But in some ways, it is easier to go on a mission trip right after a hurricane, when the devastation is acute, the pain is in the news, and the images rise above the noise. But what is transformative for us in this work is that we are continuing to develop and deepen our Gulf Coast relationships two years later. We made a conscious decision to return to Mississippi again this summer, three years after the storm, because what we've experienced in America is that issues raised by the storm's devastation have started to recede in the national consciousness. The lay and ordained leaders of St. Andrew's are making an intentional choice to keep our community in Massachusetts connected to the folks on the Gulf coast for whom this is a ten- to twenty-year recovery effort. To that end, we maintain a sister parish relationship with Christ Church, Bay St. Louis. It's not just about doing the work of rebuilding, but realizing we are connected to this other community. As a congregation we want to continue to live into this relationship."

Chris speaks with eagerness about this work, his face alive with joy as he describes an inclusive Christianity where all are welcome at the metaphorical banquet table of the family of God. "My family's kind of 'open table' was formative for me," he says. "It was a wonderful lesson to learn from my parents."

Chris wants to bring everyone to the table, to build relationships across socioeconomic barriers by forming community, the beloved community, at the table of abundant blessing. Getting to the table, he believes, has everything to do with telling our stories and recognizing our identity within the matrix of human relationships.

"The disparity of rich and poor is very apparent and very visible even when you live in communities that you'd assume are homogenously wealthy, like the one I grew up in, because you see people at different levels of the economic spectrum in your daily life. The rich may never see where the poor live, but they interact with them daily. The working poor see the rich every day. The question is, how do you respond to the disparity?"

For those in the "upper bands" of the spectrum of wealth—that is, anyone with education, work, enough to eat, and a place to sleep—Chris sees three possible choices.

"First," he says, "There is denial. You can deny that the poor exist, you can turn your back. You can reduce yourself to living only within your own economic band; you can keep with 'your kind.' You can say: 'I do the best I can within my band.'

"A second possibility is that you are unable to deny the difference in economic disparity but you don't know how to engage it. You are aware of inequality, you are aware of suffering, and you experience a sense of responsibility for this system in which you see the suffering of many. You know that you are not 'the many,' but you don't know how implicated to feel, how responsible for it you are. This whole can of worms can be overwhelming—you can choose whether to enter or not, so you choose not to."

"But there is another possibility, a third way," he says. "You can respond with awareness to the spectrum of suffering—identification with people who are suffering to the point that you can't choose not to be implicated. This identification is the opposite of guilt or shame. It is rooted in a sense of solidarity with everyone who suffers at the hands of forces they cannot control—in the recognition that we are part of everyone.

"I think Christianity invites us into that third way of being. It's a way of being connected, a way of starting to close the distance in life experience between our own sufferings and the sufferings of the poor. It's acknowledging that suffering is real and I'm part of it: both creating it and experiencing it. I call that third way 'poverty of spirit.' I want to help wealthy persons understand this third way so that they don't jump back to denial or think that they have a choice about getting involved.⌈I want to help people get from step two to step three, to see that as members of the human family we don't really have a choice but to acknowledge our connections to each other."⌉

Taking this step requires a new understanding of abundance and scarcity.

"In affluent American communities, it is often the case that our material abundance creates a kind of spiritual poverty in which the sufferings of life cannot be acknowledged and God's blessings cannot be celebrated or cherished," Chris says. "There is instead an anxiety, a fear that what we have today will be gone tomorrow. There is a fear that we're not doing enough to protect ourselves or to give our children an advantage. This outlook leads to a spirituality of scarcity—where we cling tightly to what we have, unable to embrace God's transforming mercy, unable to trust that there is enough for all. Holding on to what we've got keeps us from moving beyond charity to advocacy, moving beyond seeing the poor as 'other' to seeing ourselves in solidarity with these brothers and sisters in Christ. Holding on in fear keeps us from experiencing abundance, the abundance of God's kingdom.

"My calling is to invite people to recognize their spiritual poverty *and* start telling stories not only about their affluence but also about their need. That's the first step toward justice."

But it's not an easy step, he acknowledges. "Taking this step wounds your spirit," he says. "This wound of knowledge really connects you to some kind of experience of suffering, some lack or need or hunger that you don't have as a wealthy person, a hunger that takes you to the edge of survival. Telling your story—saying out loud what's really going on instead of saying 'everything's fine'—makes you vulnerable. It wounds your spirit and it transforms your soul. It's an 'aha' moment that takes you out of yourself, out of your comfort zone, and then you can see that you are part of the beloved community—you enter a wider band of the spectrum than you ever thought you could be part of."

One such "aha" moment for Chris occurred in Bethlehem at Christmas time.

"When I was in seminary I went on pilgrimage to the Holy Land. We arrived in Bethlehem on the night of Orthodox Christmas (our Epiphany) and we went straight to a celebration in this Palestinian Christian community, Beit Sahour. The party began at 10:00 at night and lasted until 4:00 or 5:00 in the morning. The amount of celebration and unmitigated joy was incredible! Children screaming with glee, men embracing, women dancing. I'd never seen anything like it!

"In order to get to Beit Sahour we had to go through checkpoint after checkpoint—and while our American passports made the experience only mildly inconvenient, simply by looking out the windows of our bus, the hardship of others at these checkpoints was all around us, unavoidable. As our time in the West Bank went on, we heard story after story of lost jobs, harassment, power outages, lack of medical supplies—a life of material scarcity.

"And yet this community was still capable of this incredible celebration of Christmas. I watched their ability to celebrate abundant life, despite their pain and suffering, and to do so far beyond the ways that I had celebrated abundant life living in a rich country. I saw incredible joy next to incredible suffering. The suffering is real, and the joy is also real.

"Most often, you can close your door, turn off your computer, mute your TV; you can say 'no' to the people who are on the other side of those news stories. In the middle of that Christmas celebration, I wasn't able to do that. I was on their side of the news stories. I could see their suffering and their joy, all at once. And I knew my own country was in some way responsible for that suffering. We don't celebrate Christmas in America the way they do in Beit Sahour. And as I felt my own poverty of spirit there, I somehow found a piece of abundant life that I had been missing.

"This is about the experience of being part of a beloved community," he says, "not just being beloved as an individual. Congregations can talk a lot about how God loves you, but it's only good if we see that God loves us all—and wants us to love each other."

God's love for all, the beloved community, is revealed in the beatitudes, says Chris. "The real purpose of the beatitudes is to reveal the solidarity among all people, despite the vast differences in human circumstances on this planet. The beatitudes aren't just about 'those other people' who are different because they are poor or hungry or persecuted. They are also about how our own lives are made spiritually poor by the suffering of others."

This global solidarity was the focus of a seminary project for Chris. He and his classmates in The Beatitudes Society at Episcopal Divinity School designed a week of chapel services that drew attention to the United Nation's Millennium Development Goals (MDGs).

"We were riffing off of Bono's statement at the 2006 National Prayer Breakfast that the MDGs are really beatitudes for the globalized world," he says. "We paired one beatitude with each of the MDGs; we created interactive stations for each of these pairs, and we capped off the week with a U2charist. We matched 'blessed are the poor in spirit' with the eighth MDG—'forming global partnerships for development'—recognizing our own poverty as a force for solidarity.

"As followers of Christ, we have an unbreakable relationship with those who are persecuted, suffering, or destitute. Their material poverty reveals our own spiritual poverty. They are poor, so we are poor. Often we choose not to recognize the relationship between the immensity of poverty in the world and our spiritual incompleteness. But in the beatitudes, Jesus challenges that kind of denial of involvement or self-removal from a world of suffering."

Chris likens the challenge of the beatitudes to Caravaggio's painting *The Entombment of Christ*.

"At first glance it seems like a story about other people tending to the wounded body of Christ—there is all this care and pain and drama going on, but it is in the painting's space. The viewer observes this, but does not participate. But as you stare at the canvas more, you realize that you, the viewer, are part of the painting. Because of the perspective that Caravaggio used, it becomes clear that the men holding Jesus are about to throw Christ's body into the viewer's space. Suddenly we are no longer detached bystanders observing a work of art, but we are about to enter the painting. Or more precisely, the reality of the painting is about to enter our reality. It's not our choice; we are about to receive Christ's body and become part of the Body of Christ. Denial or detachment is no longer possible. Like the beatitudes, the painting is not a story about Christ and someone else. It's about how Christ unites those who suffer or mourn with those who have been watching from the sidelines. Whether we are ready or not, now we are in relationship with God. Now we touch the suffering of the world. They are poor, so we are poor.

"This is *ubuntu*," says Chris, using the African expression that says "I am a person through other persons."

"I want people to experience ubuntu, to be transformed in their souls," Chris says. "I want them to discover their spiritual poverty underneath their material wealth, I want them to discover the abundance—the joy, the kingdom of heaven—that comes from coming to the table to share first our stories and then ourselves."

REFLECTION

The first one is the hardest one. Matthew's version of the beatitudes raises all kinds of questions, especially this first one. For starters, why does Matthew say "blessed are the poor in spirit" instead of "blessed are the poor," as Luke records it? Is Matthew the "spiritualized version" of the beatitudes as many scholars contend? And how about the matter of heaven and the questions about time and space? What is heaven anyway? Where is heaven, and when?

These questions matter. They matter of course to the scripture scholars who research and write and debate about the collection of Jesus' sayings that we call the beatitudes, and they also matter to the rest of us who want to live the beatitudes in the twenty-first century.

They matter if we want to discover the kind of abundance that Chris Wendell describes above, to move beyond our anxiety into new relationship with God and each other.

It's our questions, I believe, that lead us into the heart of the Jesus story, and that can lead us into the heart of our own stories. All the Gospel accounts resound with questions, from "Who do you say that I am?" and "What do you seek?" to the question on the dying Jesus' lips, "My God, my God why have you forsaken me?" In the questions we can hear the echo of our own doubt, and we can discover the stirrings of an Easter faith, "Why do you seek the living among the dead?" and of an Easter commitment, "Do you love me?"

As a wisdom teacher, Jesus taught his disciples with puzzling parables, pithy aphorisms, and challenging questions, inviting them to discover a new way of living by engaging his many questions. When the young lawyer asked what he had to do to inherit eternal life, Jesus did not recite the law, but answered Semitic-style with yet another question and proceeded to lead the lawyer through more questioning into his story of the good Samaritan. The story turned upside down the conventional wisdom of the day about the limits of neighbor love, inviting the lawyer and all of us listeners ever since to expand our own capacity for compassion (Luke 10:25–37).

Conventional wisdom also gets turned upside down in the beatitudes by Jesus daring to name the poor, the meek, and the mournful as the blessed ones. What could be blessed about poverty or grief? Is this simply the promise of a better day by and by, when we die? Do the beatitudes describe some future reward for suffering now? If blessing is a good thing, it would seem that common sense, and the economic and political norms of first-century Palestine

(and twenty-first-century America) tell us that the wealthy
bear the signs of blessing, and the powerful, not the meek,
own the earth today and will keep it tomorrow. So what
kind of blessing is there, and who are the poor in spirit?
What is Jesus talking about?

This first beatitude gives us the opportunity to
take a look at Jesus and his Jewish tradition and those
phrases "blessed are," "poor in spirit," and "kingdom of
heaven"—all of which are important for understanding
the rest of the beatitudes.

Jesus and His Jewish Roots

Matthew wants his Jewish listeners to recognize Jesus'
roots in their tradition. Not only does he begin his account
with a genealogy confirming Jesus' Jewish heritage, Matthew also shapes his account of the life of Jesus into five
sections, just as the Torah includes five books (Genesis,
Exodus, Leviticus, Numbers, Deuteronomy). With the
words "Jesus . . . went up the mountain . . . and taught
them," Matthew reminds his listeners of Moses and Sinai
(vv. 1–2). Just as Moses went up Mount Sinai and gave
the people the Ten Commandments, Jesus goes up the
new mountain and offers the new teaching. Matthew
presents Jesus and his several sayings as the fulfillment
of the prophets and of Israel. Matthew's Jesus takes his
place as the new prophet, the new Moses.

Both Moses and Jesus offer the people of Israel a new
way of living that countered the dominant order of day,
from the empires of Egypt to Babylon to Rome. Just as
Moses' commandments were practices that fostered just
communities and protected the most vulnerable, Jesus'
sayings are words of deliverance intended to express

God's care for the ones in need.[1] Keeping Sabbath guaranteed rest for exploited workers; recognizing the meek rather than the mighty located God not in the emperor's palace but in the widow's outstretched hand.

This new prophet Jesus, Matthew clues in his listeners, is one who shows us the presence of God. Matthew tells this not directly, but by the quotations he uses from Isaiah, words that the prophet used to describe the presence of God. In telling the stories of Jesus' birth and baptism, his travels throughout the Galilee, his healing the sick and calling disciples, Matthew sets the stage for the beatitudes and the Sermon on the Mount by giving us phrases straight from Isaiah, announcing that God is doing something entirely new in Jesus. God's Spirit is present in the one called Emmanuel, "God with us" (Isa. 7:14; Matt. 1:23) and the One claimed as God's Beloved at his baptism in the Jordan (Isa. 42:1; Matt. 3:17). John the Baptist announces God's liberating justice with the words from Isaiah 40: "Prepare the way of the Lord, make his paths straight" (Matt. 3:3). And the people in Galilee are described with words from Isaiah 8 and 9: "The people who [have been living] in darkness have seen a great light, and for those who sat in the shadow of death light has dawned" (Matt. 4:16). Take note, Matthew is saying, the good news of God's liberating justice is breaking through in our day in Jesus of Nazareth.

"Blessed Are"

The good news begins with a blessing. There are many translations of the Greek word for blessing, *makarios,* that show up in various translations of the Bible: "blest," "how blest," "happy," "fortunate," "joyful," or "congratulations." Some of these translations describe an individual subjective state of mind (such as "happy") that seems to me to miss the point of Jesus' teaching. Being blessed is not the same as being happy. In these sayings, Jesus is teaching us something about God and what's important to God. With the word "blessed," Jesus is signaling (as the prophet Isaiah did before him), "God cares about this" or "God commends this."[2] This is not so much an evaluation—that poverty is good—as it is an invitation to shift our own perspective on what we might consider a blessing; we are invited to participate in God's transformation of our world. Look at it this way, Jesus is saying. This is what God commends: our alliance with the poor, the meek, the peacemaker, and the persecuted. The good news and blessing, Jesus announces, is that we are invited into a new way of joining with God in creating the kind of world God wants everyone to inhabit.

"The Poor in Spirit"

The first word of good news is for the poor: blessed are the poor in spirit. But why the lengthy "blessed are the poor in spirit" and not simply "blessed are the poor" as we see in Luke's version of the beatitudes (Luke 6:20)? The answer lies in Isaiah 61:1: "The Spirit of the Lord is upon me . . . to preach good news to the poor." We hear the same quotation in Luke's account of Jesus' first sermon at Nazareth (Luke 4:18). Isaiah uses the Hebrew word for poor, *anawim*, the poorest of the poor, those whose material poverty has broken their spirit.[3] Whether recorded by Luke or Matthew, Jesus' sayings about the poor have their origin in Isaiah.

To say that the poor are blessed is not to say that they are morally superior or somehow noble because of their poverty, neither is it to romanticize grinding poverty as some kind of happy simplicity. Nor is it to say that the poor are blessed because there is some "special place in heaven" for those who suffer. The poor are called blessed because God's first concern is for the poor and the oppressed, as the Hebrew Scriptures say in so many different voices and so many different calls for justice, from Exodus to Zephaniah: "I dwell with those who are contrite and humble in spirit, to revive the spirit of the humble and to revive the heart of the contrite" (Isa. 57:15). "If the one who is poor cries to me, I will hear, for I am compassionate" (Exod. 22:27 rsv). The prophets' voicing of God's passion for the least among us echoes throughout all accounts of the Jesus story: in his parables, his acts of healing, and his unorthodox hospitality for the outcast. We hear this description of "what matters most" summarized in Matthew 25, about God's imperative that we feed the hungry, give water to the thirsty, clothe the naked, visit the sick, and welcome the stranger: "As you did it to one of the least of these . . . you did it to me" (v. 40). The poor in spirit are indeed the least of these.

"The Kingdom of Heaven"

Jesus' mission, like that of the prophets before him, was to announce the good news of God's kingdom. This kingdom is a real time kingdom, a kingdom of this world. That is not to say, of course, that this kingdom is a place, a kingdom with a king and armies and flags. It is not an otherworldly, spiritual kingdom of the future. To speak of the kingdom of God is to speak of the presence of God, or the reign of God, whenever and wherever that may be (which of course does not exclude the future).

In Glen Stassen's expression, the kingdom of God is a "happening."[4] It is an experience of God present in this world, and we know it when we see it. The prophet Isaiah describes the kingdom as the presence of God, and the attributes of that divine presence include Spirit, light, liberating justice, peace, healing, joy, and return from exile. These are the signs of God's presence that Matthew employs at the beginning of his story of Jesus.[5] And these are the signs of God's presence that we can see in our world, whenever we see healing or joy or peace or liberation from oppression.

When we see that this is a kingdom both "not of this world" and also something very earthly and very political, we can see what a powerful manifesto these beatitudes are. This kingdom is a sanctuary where all are welcome, all are equal, all are nourished. Some scripture scholars translate kingdom as "kin-dom," from the Greek *basileia,* a household, where people live in mutual care, free from patriarchal hierarchy. This kind of kingdom announced by Jesus throughout the Gospels is an affront to Caesar's realm and rule, and to any kingdom "of this world" with kings and princes and warriors, along with their slaves and serfs and underlings. This new kingdom, this new reign of God, stands in opposition to the dominating powers of this earth from Pharaoh to Caesar and any empire since. As Marcus Borg wrote, Jesus inverted the notions of kingdoms of his day and instead announced "what life would be like on earth if God were Lord and the lords of this earth were not."[6]

If we were to describe this kingdom, we would use those same words that describe the experience of the presence of God: we would use those key words from Isaiah, words like light, peace, healing, joy, and deliverance from exile. We could say that it is a place where God's passion for justice and God's concern for the poor are realized, and everyone has enough. This kingdom is a place where compassion is not limited to personal relationships but is in fact the fabric of social and political life. But if we are really talking about something that could happen here, on this earth, in this lifetime, then why are we talking about heaven?

Matthew used the term *heaven*. As a Jew writing for Jews, Matthew was observing his tradition's custom of refraining from the use of the name of God, and therefore called the kingdom of God the kingdom of heaven. The kingdom of heaven is the same as the kingdom of God named by Mark and Luke. Unfortunately, Matthew's use of the term *heaven* in the beatitudes has caused generations of Christians to presume that these sayings of Jesus describe a world to come rather than the world we inhabit. Hearing these words as descriptive of our world allows us to hear good news for the oppressed and good news for all of us, as we are invited to participate in God's life, God's justice, and God's politics.

Responding to the Invitation

In Chris Wendell's story, his church's work in building both houses and relationships on the Mississippi Gulf Coast is a response to this beatitude's invitation to participate in God's justice. Through his story, Chris has struggled with something with which all of us struggle, I think—some measure of guilt. Now some guilt, perhaps, in is order, especially as we look at the appetite for consumption (some have called it "affluenza") that infects our North American culture and affects our globalized economy. But Chris's third way, I believe, moves us beyond feeling immobilizing guilt to being engaged in meaningful action, enabling each of us to find a way to participate with the many who suffer from economic poverty.

Chris's third way makes me think of the teachings of Latin American liberation theologians and their understanding of "God's preferential option for the poor" that calls Christians to stand in solidarity with the poor and against inhumane poverty.[7] God is not calling us simply to "do good works," as Peruvian theologian Gustavo Gutiérrez emphasizes:

> The preferential option for the poor is ultimately a question of friendship. Without friendship, an option for the poor can easily become commitment to an abstraction (to a social class, a race, a culture, an idea). Aristotle emphasized the important place of friendship for the moral life, but we also find this clearly stated in John's Gospel. Christ says, "I do not call you servants, but friends." As Christians, we are called to reproduce this quality of friendship in our relationships with others. When we become friends with the poor, their presence leaves an indelible imprint on our lives, and we are much more likely to remain committed.[8]

Now, God's option for the poor is not something that makes us exactly comfortable—and Isaiah, Amos, and Jesus probably didn't intend it to! When we see those who make this option the focus of their lives, we often see larger-than-life heroes or saints whose commitments and lifestyles don't exactly make us comfortable either. But I know I need those heroes to inspire me to extend my reach a little, to look beyond my own comfort to a world of need. One such hero for me is physician Paul Farmer. Harvard-educated and Haiti-based, Farmer is relentless in his work to bring basic health care to the world's poor, and makes no bones about his "O for the P" (his short-hand version of preferential Option for the Poor). He has found resonance in liberation theology, which he calls "a powerful rebuke to the hiding away of poverty."[9]

Most of us don't have the singular passion of a Paul Farmer, or a Dorothy Day, or any saint or martyr we might name. That's one reason we single out these few for sainthood. But the communion of saints is all of us, all of us who love God, and we all play a part in God's dream of justice. We are all invited to find our way to respond to God's invitation to care for this world.

As we respond to the invitation, we can move from the fear and anxiety of our carefully guarded scarcity and discover abundance, the abundance illustrated by Jesus in his story of the "one who had more than all of them":

> He sat down opposite the treasury, and watched the crowd putting money into the treasury. Many rich people put in large sums. A poor widow came and put in two small copper coins, which are worth a penny. Then he called his disciples and said to them, "Truly I tell you, this poor widow has put in more than all those who are contributing to the treasury. For all of them have contributed out of their abundance; but she out of her poverty has put in everything she had, all she had to live on"(Mark 12:41-44).

As this widow discovers, finding our way costs us something. To follow this way, to find abundance, calls us to place allegiance in something other than the safe conventions of the day, something other than our paychecks or our degrees or our pedigrees. The people who heard these beatitudes of Jesus knew that. They knew the legend of their ancestors' exodus from Egypt. They knew that a relationship with God required choice; they knew their ancestors' choice for the promised land meant that they had to leave the binding but secure chains of slavery for the risk of freedom. They knew their ancestors had to leave the certainty of the gods they had constructed out of stone and clay to follow a god they could not see. They knew it would cost everything, this way of abundance.

As this widow knew, their choice to follow Jesus into the new reign of God, the new kingdom, demands far more than coins offered to the temple treasury; it demands transformation from the inside out. They heard the words of Jesus, "Blessed are the poor in spirit for theirs is the kingdom of heaven" and Moses' words, "choose life," echoed in their hearts.

And these words echo in our hearts. Choose life, we hear Jesus say. Discover the blessing of this new way. This will not be convenient. It will transform everything. But it will show you heaven, this way of abundance.

To be a disciple of Jesus in first-century Palestine meant giving up all the conventions of Jewish village life and temple teaching. It meant a new kind of hardship, not the same desert trek of those ancestors set free from Pharaoh, for the challenge of Jesus would lead to the cross. Even as the disciples heard the promise of blessing, of the kingdom of heaven placed right in their midst, they all knew the danger of this new way of Jesus.

They could hear Jesus say, "This road will be a hard one, a long one, and I can only promise you one thing: God's enduring love. Everything else can crumble. I cannot give you victory over the Romans, I cannot assure you that the temple will stand. It won't. All I can offer you is enduring love. So come my way; but know that you must give up everything for this kingdom of heaven I bring."

Absurd words to a people that had struggled from before memory to survive, struggled for stability in the face of drought and foreign occupations, struggled against extinction. Why risk it all? What blessing could there be in this new kingdom, this new way?

We might ask the same questions in the twenty-first century. We are not too different from those first-century people. We like stability, security. We like to see our problems solved and our affairs in order. What would we risk to experience the kingdom that Jesus promises in this first beatitude and all the rest? What would happen if we let ourselves experience the kind of "wound of spirit" that Chris is talking about, the moments that take us out of our comfort zone and into new relationships in the beloved community? What would happen if we allowed that all-embracing love of God to begin to work in us and among us? Whom might we befriend? Whom might we offend?

If we decide to look at the life and ministry of Jesus, if we decide to listen to the beatitudes, the parables, the stories of the Bible, it might mean that we find ourselves at the margins of conventional behavior, perhaps at the edges of those "bands" that Chris names. The way that Jesus announces is the way that throws privilege aside for the radical embrace of the one at the margins. The way that Jesus announces says that our Sunday worship and our everyday ethics and our real life politics, our practices and habits and institutions, must never serve the end of privilege or domination. To choose the new kingdom way of Jesus means to question the prevailing forces in our culture: the violence, the affluence, the individualism.

The way of Jesus announced in the beatitudes asks us to be ready for change, asks us to face into the direction of the new and untried to build the beloved community. The collection of biblical stories, from the ancient legends of Moses and Pharaoh to the parable of the widow and her mite to these sayings that we call the beatitudes, all of them say that we cannot stand fast in what we call our habitual convictions: we can only take that leap of faith, trusting in the paradox of a loving God's embrace, an embrace that sets us free for abundance and for blessing, free to be "poor in spirit," free as the widow and her mite.

FOR FURTHER REFLECTION

 1. In Chris's story, he speaks of an "aha moment" that took him beyond his comfort zone to an awareness of others. When have you had such a moment? Can you describe it?

 2. What do you think of Chris's description of the "bands" that define and separate us? Where do you see yourself in these bands?

 3. What do you think of the idea of heaven as "both very earthly and very political"? In what ways do you agree and differ?

4. What in your experience can you describe that looks like the kingdom of heaven, the presence of God?

5. Heroes like Paul Farmer and his "O for the P" set the bar quite high for all of us. Often, when we learn the personal stories of such heroes (Martin Luther King, Jr., and Dorothy Day, for example) we find that their lives demand more sacrifice (of family relationships, personal comfort, safety, health) than we are willing to make. How do you feel about such heroes? Who are your heroes?

CHAPTER TWO

Blessed are those who mourn

"Blessed are those who mourn,
for they will be comforted."—Matthew 5:4

STEFANI'S STORY

Stefani laughs easily, a deep, throaty chuckle. Her eyes sparkle. Her middle name could be Joy. But she says, "What a sad world. I look around the world and grieve."

Stefani is not a sad person, but she has the capacity to grieve, and she has done a good bit of grieving in her recent work as an Episcopal priest. A few years out from seminary, Stefani Schatz has recently been serving as a priest in a working-class parish in Manchester, in the Midlands of England. She moved there with her husband Joe, also an Episcopal priest, so that Joe could pursue his doctoral studies at the University of Manchester. Once the hub of the Industrial Revolution, and the home of Rolls Royce, Manchester is now slowly recovering from economic depression.

"I work with people who have no jobs, and whose families for two or three generations have had no jobs. These are people who are living on the dole. They are called "unwaged," chronically unwaged. These are people who can't afford to move anywhere else. I see people who die here at a younger age than other places because of alcoholism, drugs, and their overall hard lives.

I see older people staying on while their homes crumble around them. The region is depressed, the people are depressed.

"There is no sense of hope. So many people believe that nothing will change, nothing will get better," she said. "This feeling pervades everything."

Stefani does a lot of funerals, at least one every week. Far outnumbering the baptisms and the weddings in her church, the funerals underscore the sense of loss that pervades the neighborhoods, but they have given her a close connection with her neighbors and a new affirmation of what it means to be the church.

Central to Stefani's understanding of church is that it be a place of welcome and inclusion. She remembers the welcome a group of older women in a nearby pew once extended to her, when she was returning to church after her college years. "Barbara Kelley took me aside one week after I'd been attending regularly and asked if I'd like to help her with the altar guild set up/clean up and doing the reading or prayers. I remember her telling me about the prayerful 'work' we were doing behind the scenes but also beyond the words was her lovely incarnation of that as well," says Stefani. "The welcome came in her noticing me, then asking me to help, and her gentle guidance in that help. She called herself 'old' and wanted to pass along her knowledge and love of the altar guild ministry to someone younger and was very intentional about it with me."

Stefani knows that it matters to offer that same kind of hospitality to anyone who walks through the church doors. She is known for her warmth, her generous welcoming spirit, and her unabashed commitment to an "open" communion table. When she presides at communion, she issues an open invitation to all to share in the bread and wine, saying "This is God's table, and all are welcome!" In Manchester, with all the funerals, she's seen that welcome reach outside the church doors.

"I'm asking myself, 'What is the church?' Is it that building? That Sunday? Or is it these people who are making a connection with God? Particularly in preparation for funerals, I'm constantly hearing the faith journeys of people who are outside the church. I meet them, I spend an hour with them, I listen to them. I write a vignette of their lives, just a few words to say at the funeral, but words that they haven't heard in church before. My care for them is to tell this story, to give their lives back to them, affirmed by God and the community.

"They say crazy things about the future, about angels, about how their loved one is not dead but gone to sleep, but they still find ways to comfort each other," Stefani says. "When we get to the chapel, in the space of the church, I see men cry, I see them touch, I see the people comforting each other. Submerged in the mourning, I see such joy. God is in that."

The joy comes when the mourners are able to hear that God meets them right where they live. God isn't locked up in church, available only on Sunday mornings or only with the right words or the right behavior. "God meets them," Stefani says, "in the real and in the local. That's the beatitude. That's the blessing. That's comfort right here and now."

Stefani recalls a funeral that relocated her sense of church. "I got a call about a man who had died. Roy was living on his pension, and he died at home, all alone.

But he left two names to call. I called these two numbers and reached two women who told me the story of this man. They knew nothing about his biography, they just knew him from the pub where they were waitresses. They talked to me about his ways, his speech, his kidding, his favorite meals, how he would nap on his stool and then wake up and ask, 'Why is my beer flat?' They both told the stories of his life as they had heard him tell them.

"When we did his funeral in the church, I told them, 'You are his family.' At that moment I felt like I was naming to them the value that they had, that they were God's being in the world because they were this man's family. They were the mourners, but they were comforted because they were called family. It made them feel less alone too.

"And when the funeral was over they said to me: 'Come to the pub.'

"These were words of comfort to me: 'Come to the pub.' They took me in as their family, too. They showed me that God was in the pub. The church is in that real, local world, wherever we need comfort. That's where God is, and that's where the church needs to be."

Stefani is aware that what she sees on the streets of Manchester is what she could see on the streets of rust belt or rural America, anyplace that's been hit by hard times. "Manchester's given me eyes to see things in my own country I couldn't see before," she says.

"I meet so many sad people who die of such loneliness. What a sad world. I look around the world and grieve. There are so many people walking around with their personal grief. Sometimes it's week-old grief, or two-week-old grief, or year-old grief, or a lifetime of grief. When you see the amount of people always losing people they love, and then multiply that to the problems of the world—" Stefani stops.

"I open up the newspaper and I have the whole world at my fingerprints, the state of the planet. There is plenty to mourn in our world, isn't there?

"You know, at the opening of every funeral, I stand up and I look into the eyes of the people that are there and I say: 'Blessed are those who mourn, for they will be comforted.' And you know something? I say it with conviction that it's the truth. I believe it.

"Manchester—this social location, these people—has burned upon my heart something that I'll always be able to translate to any place I serve: It's a Good Friday world we live in. But God will be there in the mourning and in the comforting. It's this Good Friday God that I see every day that makes me value and be able to preach Easter morning."

REFLECTION

Some years ago, the expression "Life's a beach" was going around. It drove me crazy, the same way the saying "Don't worry, be happy" drove me crazy. Currently, I get peeved when I hear "It's all good." Life is not a beach and it's not "all good."

Life is hard. I don't mean to be such a scrooge, but anyone who is conscious and has a conscience must admit it's a tough world out there, and people live with all sorts of tragedies. Life is hard. The people in Stefani Schatz's Manchester parish know this, and I imagine that those who gather nightly for a pint at Joe's pub are not saying "Life's a beach." They gather for a bit of relief at the end of a hard day. They gather to break up the boredom of empty hours or to ease the pain of aching backs and broken dreams. But they do gather. [They gather for comfort—] and not just the comfort of brewed hops but the comfort of communion. They make a kind of church together, as Stefani discovered, a kind of church that isn't bound by stone walls and stained glass.

I imagine it's the kind of church the very earliest Christians made when they first gathered with their friend Jesus for a feast of bread and fish and stories. It's the kind of church they made later, when they huddled in upper rooms, fearful and brokenhearted after the crucifixion. Maybe, gathered there after he was gone, one of them remembered Jesus' aphorism, "Blessed are those who mourn, for they will be comforted." And maybe these words reminded them who they were and what the presence of God could mean in their lives and in their world. Maybe remembering these words helped them remember to pass the bread and wine around and make communion and keep on being community.

When the followers of Jesus first heard him say "Blessed are those who mourn," they knew this saying made good sense along with the words "Blessed are the poor in spirit" because they knew themselves to be poor. Even on the best of days, they had plenty to grieve as people who suffered multiple injustices under Rome's boot. Two-thirds of all they produced from the fields and herds and fishing nets they were forced to turn over to the ruling classes. They had little to show for their hard labors. They had very little comfort.

But when they heard Jesus say, "Blessed are those who mourn, for they will be comforted," they heard the echo of

the prophet Isaiah and the promise that the ashes of their
sorrow would become garlands, and that the oil of glad-
ness would ease their mourning (Isa. 61:3). Some might
have heard balm for their individual sadness, but they also
heard the prophet's announcement of the kingdom of God
in their midst. They knew that Jesus spoke in the tradition
of the prophets, concerned for the people's well-being.
Their suffering is acknowledged by the one who speaks for
God, the one who announces God's presence and God's
blessing. Jesus joins them in their suffering, and the new
kingdom is at hand.

Jesus' words of blessing and comfort describe the new
way of God, and so do his actions. Time and again in the
four Gospel accounts, Jesus is present at the scene of suffering and he acknowledges and participates in mourning.
In his presence and in his action the experience of grief
becomes a window to the kingdom of God, where joy and
healing are possible. But when he acts, something happens
to all who are gathered, and that, I think, is the key to the
kingdom, or at least the key to living this beatitude. Two
stories in particular give us these keys: the story of the
raising of Jairus's daughter and the story of the raising of
Lazarus.

Jairus's young daughter is near death.[1] He is frightened,
grief stricken, and desperate. He seeks out the traveling
healer from Nazareth, falls at his feet, and begs him for
his healing touch. As together they make their way back
to Jairus's house, word comes that the girl is already dead.
Nonetheless, Jesus continues with Jairus.

With him, Jesus brings his friends, Peter and James and
John, and he brings the girl's mother and father. They all
gather at that bedside. This is not a solo act. In response

to the father's faith, the mother's presence, in the name of God, and with the hope of the people, Jesus calls to the girl and she gets up and walks. He gathers together at that bedside the ones who care for her and charges them with her comfort and provision: to feed the girl and carry on the healing and comforting work he has begun.

Healing takes place in community. In the story of Jesus, healing and caring and comforting cannot be found without community gathered around.

That is what Stefani has discovered in the people of Manchester, in meeting their grief, entering their stories, and offering them communion. It is what she discovered when first returning to church after college, and it's the hospitality she seeks to extend as she brings the church beyond the stained glass and into the pub and the larger community, the kind of comfort announced by Jesus, the comfort of the presence of God, the new kingdom of God.

There is a sign of this new kingdom in the familiar Lazarus story, to be sure, a sign of the presence of God and a promise of life that defies death, but there's an edge to the promise. Before the promise is a clear directive: "Unbind him and let him go free." The promise of life comes right alongside a call to act, a call to community.

It all starts with Martha. Martha is the key to John's story of Lazarus, a story not found in the other three Gospels, a story filled with unexpected twists and turns (see John 11:1–57). In Jesus' exchange with Martha, John gives us the first clue that something new is afoot. Martha goes out to the road to meet Jesus. Her audacity was bolder even than that of the Samaritan woman at the well: Jewish women did not speak to men on the road, they certainly did not speak first, and they only spoke if spoken to.

Martha is a good Jewish woman, but she is audacious in her anger and grief: "If you had been here my brother would not have died," she declares. Jesus rises to the occasion with equal audacity: "Your brother will rise," he insists.

At first, she thinks he is talking about some kind of *future* resurrection, the kind of resurrection the Pharisees believed in. No news in that.

But then comes the clincher, the last of the famous "I am" statements that punctuate John's version of the Jesus story. After a series of statements—I am the bread of life, I am the light of the world, I am the good shepherd—we hear Jesus say to Martha: "I am the resurrection and the life."

"I am the resurrection and the life," he says. "Do you believe me?"

Martha doesn't hesitate. "Yes, Lord I believe."

Martha's proclamation of faith announces the wholly unexpected, the wholly new, the impossible, in the face of death. Lest there be any misunderstanding about the radical nature of the transformation from the old ways of death to the new way of life, John reminds his listeners of the teaching of the rabbis which said that after a person died, his or her life breath hovered near the body for three days and then left; by the fourth day, the soul was gone. Everyone knew there could be no hope for life on the fourth day, no possibility of resuscitation. Lazarus is gone, long gone. And Jesus weeps. He joins the grieving. John's Gospel doesn't say so, but if this Jesus story matches up with everything else about Jesus, his weeping with the grieving ones is what makes possible his next words and indeed the whole story:

"Lazarus, come out!"

Lazarus is alive—not in some kind of afterlife, but in the flesh and blood, here and now.

What to do with this impossible new life? Worship the miracle worker? No, get busy. "Unbind him and let him go!" Jesus commands, calling on the community around Lazarus to carry on with the tasks of living. Now, John could have had Jesus do the unbinding, completing himself the miraculous task of bringing Lazarus back. But the raising of Lazarus—even in the Gospel of John that is so set on showing the miraculous—is not so much about a divine supernatural intervention as it is about the power of the gathered community.

Divinity is present, to be sure, in the One who is himself called Life and Resurrection. But it takes the entire community together with Jesus to create new life, as we see with Jairus's daughter.

When Jesus tells them to unbind Lazarus, it is all of them, from bold Martha and the curious bystanders to the skeptical ones who did not see Jesus as the Way to new life, who are invited to join in giving life back to Lazarus.

The work of unbinding or healing or comforting or challenging or questioning cannot be done without community. I believe that's what made it possible for those first disciples to leave their fishing nets and take to the highway with Jesus: they saw the possibility of a new kind of community. They were invited by Jesus to join in a new kind of partnership that gave them an awareness of the presence of God, free from the hierarchy of the temple. And that's what made it possible for those disciples huddled in the upper room to see beyond their grief and keep moving forward to create new communities of mutual care. They were ready to be part of something larger than themselves.

This kind of community is central to living the be-atitudes. It is central to our identity as Christians as we say that God chose to become partners with us through Jesus.

Something extraordinary happens in partnership. Theologian Letty Russell, in her book *The Future of Part-nership*, called it "God's arithmetic," where one plus one equals three.[2] This is synergy: one joins with another and the energy of their union becomes greater than the sum of the parts. All who respond to the invitation of God's love find that even partnerships of two become three because of the presence of God's Spirit. Matthew gives us this in the words of Jesus, "Where two or three are gathered, there am I in the midst of them" (Matt. 18:20 RSV). And then the partnership grows, as three become more through the sharing of both need and gift.

Our gospel is a social one. The beatitudes are not a course in self-improvement; they are a description of the life we are invited to share with God and with each other, life lived in community. "Blessed are those who mourn" calls us to partnership, to be joined with God in the business of caring for all God's creatures on this planet where life is not a beach. Life is hard: 20 percent of the world's population lives splendidly on 80 percent of the world's resources, while 80 percent of our world lives on less than 2 percent of the world's resources. This is cause for mourning, but it is also a call to communion.

The stories of Jesus that gave comfort and healing and freedom to our ancestors are not stories about one isolated healing or one corpse coming back to life or one person finding enlightenment; they are stories about a whole people enlivened again. They are stories about finding the way to Easter even in a Good Friday world. These tales of truth tell about people who come to life as they are called to be life-givers, called to share the tasks of healing, comforting, raising up, giving life, building, unbinding, called to the tasks of liberation that are the signs of the new reign of God.

FOR FURTHER REFLECTION

1. One of Stefani's questions was "What is the church? Is it that building? That Sunday?" How would you answer her question? What is your experience of church? In what ways do you see the description of church changing in the future?
2. Do you agree with the view that ours is a "Good Friday" world? If so, describe times of feeling this way. What experiences of Easter have you had?
3. What have been some of your strongest experiences of community in your life? Experiences of healing? Have they been related to each other or not?
4. The author said "Our gospel is a social one." What do you think?

CHAPTER THREE

Blessed are the meek

"Blessed are the meek, for they
will inherit the earth."—Matthew 5:5

ALEX'S STORY

Alex is an intellectual. His eyes sparkle behind his thick urban-hip glasses when he talks about the life of the mind and the beloved professors that opened up for him the world of ideas.

But when he talks about his own adult reappropriation of his childhood faith, about American philosopher Richard Rorty's notion of truth, he gets excited not about a lofty philosophical perspective, but about lived-life, ground-level action.

His faith takes shape in his politics, in his networking with campus activists, his environmental work and in his blogging—he's a regular blogger at several websites, as intimately familiar with the new world of online communication as he is with the tenets of his faith. His laptop computer is plastered with decals: Question Authority, Trust Women, Demand Zero-Emission Cars.

Alex holds a thick view of religion: religion for him is not about a set of beliefs as much as it is an expression of his own heritage, identity, and location in the world. And it's about the organic meshing of religion and politics to change the world—what he calls "politics as social transformation."

"I'm a fifth generation Adventist"—that's how Alex begins a conversation about his faith. "It's what has formed me. Religion gives identity. You need to know who you are before you can change the world."

At Berkeley's Graduate Theological Union pursuing a degree in New Media, Aesthetics, and Religion, Alex's passion for theology and his vocation to teach grow out of his Adventist tradition's valuing of scholarship, but he is able to locate the first spark of passion more precisely.

For his fifteenth birthday, Alex's father gave him Blaise Pascal's *Pensées*. "I have no conversion experience to speak of, but that was the pivotal moment for me— Pascal's experience of God—it was all fire, fire. It lit my mind on fire! In reading his struggle about humility, about vanity, I began to discover you could use your mind in a religious context and create a meaningful life."

Faith for Alex is "a fertile and comforting foundation" on which to live with his doubts.

It's all about "believing, behaving, and belonging," a phrase Alex learned from one of his Adventist professors. Believing, he says, gives us what we hold to be true, and that determines our encounter with the world around us. Truth, he quotes Rorty, "is habits and tools for action." Action matters to Alex, action—or behavior—that engages the world and transforms the culture. "Behaving is about our ethics, our practice. Belonging puts us in relationships beyond the expected ones of family and friends to people around the world, to planetary belonging. Belonging gives us identity."

Belonging to the Seventh Day Adventists, Alex cares about the practice of sabbath, but the reasons to mark the seventh day have changed since childhood: "I don't practice sabbath because I think it will make God happy or worry that if I don't I will make God unhappy. I practice sabbath because it has roots in important cultural practice, in Hebrew practice.

"Abraham Joshua Heschel calls sabbath 'sanctuary in time.' That's a way I like to think about it," he says. "I'm now seeing that for the Jews sabbath was an act of justice, of reclaiming time for workers to rest from labor, a way for religious practice—behavior—to improve the lives of people. I like discovering that there's more to sabbath than being these peculiar people who go to church on Saturday."

"Blessed are the meek" speaks to Alex about believing, behaving, and belonging but it begins with belonging, with identity.

"Meekness," he says, "speaks to my masculinity."

Huh?

"It speaks directly to my identity, my understanding of what maleness means in this culture, how masculinity is created. I'm a Type A white male, taught to win a mate, to be successful, to dominate, to extract what I can from the earth. But I don't want to buy into this norm about how males behave. I want to be part of extending the meaning of maleness.

"When I hear the word *meek*," says Alex, "I think of my father. He's kind and thoughtful. I admire that. I think that's the way to be. But nothing out there in the world matches that. I get into these arguments, when I'm blogging, with these right-wing guys about immigration or terrorism—they treat compassion as if it's anti-Christian. Turning the other cheek can have a positive effect on the world. I think of meekness as nonviolence. Not violating other people. Not violating the planet. Just like there's a better way to treat people, there's a better way to treat the earth."

It's old school, he says, to think we can strip the earth to get natural resources. The change that the earth asks of us, a change in our "behaving," is possible when we look at what we believe and to whom we belong.

"I believe that God is connected to us in ways beyond human relationship; the earth is part of the body of Christ, part of God. The environment is our heritage to be passed from generation to generation; just like genes, it's our inheritance. An inheritance is not something we can earn or win; it's something that is only given to us because of relationship."

If our children and our grandchildren are to have an earth to inherit, Alex says, we must begin to practice meekness, to treat the earth with respect and value our natural resources as our heritage.

So practicing meekness, says Alex, is all about believing, behaving, and belonging: seeing God in all of creation, extending respect and compassion to each other and to the earth, and knowing our identity as members of a community of creatures who belong to each other and to the earth we call our home. Meekness begins and ends in knowing who we are: we belong to each other, to the earth itself; and we belong to God.

REFLECTION

With this beatitude, Jesus sounds the same note heard in the first two beatitudes: "Blessed are the poor in spirit" and "Blessed are those who mourn." For the third time,

Jesus locates the presence of God with the least among us, the ones without wealth, comfort, or power, the *anawim*. And for the third time, Jesus speaks in the tradition of the Hebrew prophets and echoes both Psalm 37 and Isaiah's description of God's new way where the humble shall receive the land (Ps. 37:11, Isa 61:1, 7).

The echo continues throughout the Jesus story: Matthew's gospel includes Jesus' saying about humble prayer in the Sermon on the Mount and Luke's parable of the Pharisee and the tax collector gives us a story of surprising reversal (Matt. 6:1–8, Luke 18:10–14). We see two men go up to the temple to pray: one is a respectable Pharisee, well-regarded for his pious observance of the law, and one is a despised tax collector, hated for his corrupt collaboration with Rome. The Pharisee recites his status as a righteous man and lists his commendable practices of fasting and tithing, while the tax collector cowers in the corner, begging God's mercy for his corrupt actions. No surprises here for anyone listening to the parable: Pharisees are the good guys and tax collectors are the bad guys. But Jesus turns upside down everyone's expectation, and declares the tax collector to be good in God's eyes with the words "every one who exalts himself will be humbled but he who humbles himself will be exalted."

The tax collector knows himself. He knows his need for saving grace, he knows his need for God. This beatitude is about knowing who we are. The meek named by Jesus and the prophets are not the timid or the hesitant, but rather those who are aware of their need for God. In his book *Sermon on the Mount*, Clarence Jordan pointed to two figures described as meek, Moses and Jesus, and said, "One of them defied the might of Egypt and the other couldn't be cowed by a powerful Roman official."[1]

Practicing this beatitude of meekness affords the quiet confidence of knowing who we are and whose we are. Alex is discovering this, as he identifies with the faith of his forebears (his sense of "belonging") and finds fresh ways to integrate his inherited beliefs ("believing") and practices ("behaving") with the demands of a changing world. Knowing who we are shapes the way we live in the world.

This kind of knowing of ourselves and our place in the world mattered to the ancient Hebrew prophets and the first-century Jesus movement as it matters to twenty-first-century Alex. It also mattered to a sixth-century man devoted to the alternative way of Jesus, a man who wanted to change the way the church understood itself. This man of change was Benedict of Nursia, a monk who wrote a little guidebook that has become the foundation for a practice of the Christian life. Benedict's book, now called the Rule of St. Benedict, outlines a practice of life that is, essentially, a guidebook for belonging, behaving, and believing, as Alex would put it, a guide for tending our relationship with God, with each other, and with our fragile planet.

His short book is not a theological treatise but a very simple, very direct manual for daily life in a monastery. He includes practical guidelines for the duties of the doorkeeper, the kitchen servers, and the abbot. Everyone knows his or her place, and everyone's place is honored. This guide is not a clever book of virtues or trendy seven-step guide to better living, but an alternative way that makes one virtue clear: humility. Benedict gives us the practice of humility to ground our spiritual practice.

Benedict's world was not unlike our own, a world where the (Roman) Empire of the day was crumbling.

In her discussion of the Rule of Benedict, Joan Chittister describes the sixth-century Roman world as being "a civilization in decline not unlike our own. The economy was deteriorating, the helpless were being destroyed by the warlike, the rich lived on the backs of the poor, the powerful few made decisions that profited them but plunged the powerless many into continual chaos, the empire expended more and more of its resources on militarism designed to maintain a system that, strained from within and threatened from without, was already long dead."[2]

In this environment, Benedict called for knowing our place on the earth, for a "proper sense of self in a universe of wonders," Chittister says. "Humility, in other words, is the basis for right relationships in life."[3]

Practicing this beatitude means practicing right relationships, knowing our place in the universe and our connection with God and our neighbors. "Humility," Chittister writes, "is the foundation of our relationship with God, our connectedness to others, our acceptance of ourselves, our way of using the goods of the earth and even our way of walking through the world, without arrogance, without domination, without scorn, without put-downs, without disdain, without self-centeredness. The more we know ourselves, the gentler we will be with others."[4]

Practicing "right relationship" is critically important for our planet as we move into the twenty-first century. One theologian who has helped us recall early Christianity's teaching about right relationship (as seen in Jesus' beatitudes and Benedict's humility) while pushing ahead for a twenty-first century theology is Sallie McFague. In *Life Abundant: Rethinking Theology and Economy for a Planet in Peril,* McFague makes the case for a theology of an alternative good life, an economic-ecological theology of abundance that runs counter to the pervasive North American pattern of consumer abundance. The Christian good life, she says, is marked by sustainability, self-limitation and inclusion of all, "especially the weak and vulnerable."[5] It is a theology that expresses "Blessed are the meek for they will inherit the earth" as it demands that we make a connection between our lives and the lives of everyone else on the planet, that we know our place in right relationship to God and the creation.

To practice this alternative theology of right relationship, we can borrow three tools from McFague: living cross-shaped lives, following some new house rules, and discovering wild space.

First, for North Americans Christians, McFague says, a cross-shaped life is not about what Christ does for us, but rather about what we can do for others: "We do not need so much to accept Christ's sacrifice for our sins as we need to repent of a major sin—our silent complicity in the impoverishment of others and the degradation of the planet."[6] As alternative a vision as the beatitudes of Jesus, McFague's image of the cruciform life offers the same kind of invitation to a transformed way of living. Cruciform living offers abundance through the practice, she says, of "enoughness," as we limit our consumption of the world's resources in recognition of the needs of others.

Second, we recognize the world as God's home, the place that God became and still becomes incarnate; as McFague puts it: "the 'glory' of God is not just heavenly, but earthly."[7] If the world is God's home, we should abide

by God's house rules, McFague argues. God's house rules
are not the rules of the neoclassical economic model for
individuals: you are free to amass whatever material
goods you lawfully can. If we see ourselves living in an
interconnected global village, the rules of God's house
are the rules of housemates. Housemates, operating by
an ecological economic model, abide by basic house rules:
"take only your share, clean up after yourselves and keep
the house in good repair for future occupants."[8]

But it's not easy to jump on board with cruciform
living and new house rules. Sallie McFague's ecological
theology is a reform theology, calling for a twenty-first
century reformation of our understanding of God as well
as our daily practices. This new ecological theology, like
the beatitudes, asks of us nothing less than transformation. Transformation begins with our discovery of wild
space. Wild space is that part in each one of us that does
not fit our consumer culture's definition of the good
life.

McFague invites us to discover our wild space this
way: imagine a circle. Within that circle is the dominant
cultural model: white, male, middle class, heterosexual,
educated, able bodied, Western, successful. Now, put your
own model of yourself over that circle. Some parts may
fit that dominant cultural model, some may be different.
The part of us that falls outside the conventional circle is
our wild space. Our wild space, the parts of us that do
not fit the model may be obvious: race or sex or physical
characteristics. Other parts that do not match up with
the successful conventional model may not be so obvious to others: surviving the death of a loved one, a lost
job, the struggle with addiction or depression, the vague

disappointment about not "making it," or our refusal to buy into the conventional model. Anything that causes us to question the definition of success is our wild space. Wild space is our window of opportunity to see a different vision of the good life. Being a Christian, McFague says, means having a wild space, as the Christian vision of the good life is countercultural. It is based in the generous love of God and God's desire for abundant life for all.[9]

Our wild space allows us to question the consumer model of abundance and imagine alternative ways to use the earth's resources. Our wild space allows us to question, as Alex does, the conventional definitions of masculinity or femininity and discover more egalitarian ways relate to one another. That wild space in Jesus allowed him to pose an alternative to the status quo of his day, to offer the beatitudes as a new way of living. That wild space allowed him to say that the meek are blessed, along with the poor and the mourning. The wild space in each of us allows us to question the patterns of our lives so that we might begin to live in such a way that cares for our planet and our neighbors.

Three ways: cruciform and conscious living, house rules that care for tomorrow's generations, and wild space's questioning of the status quo—all three are ways to practice this blessing of meekness, all three are ways to practice right relationship. These ways can't wait. The practice of right relationship is urgently needed in this new day of ours, this time of cataclysmic climate change and pandemic hunger and disease. The followers of the One who said "Blessed are the meek for they will inherit the earth" must lead the way, mindful of who we are and to whom we belong.

For Further Reflection

1. Alex speaks of believing, behaving, and belonging as significant for his self-knowledge. How would you describe your own sense of believing, behaving, and belonging?
2. What changes would you consider making to practice "enoughness"? What changes could your church or your school make?
3. What is your "wild space"?
4. What would it look like in your community to live by God's house rules so that all members of the household flourish?

CHAPTER FOUR

Blessed are those who hunger and thirst for justice

"Blessed are those who hunger and thirst for justice, for they will be satisfied."—Matthew 5:6

GRETA'S STORY

Greta Leach likes the sound of the beatitudes. She likes to hear that the peacemakers and the merciful and the meek are blessed. But some of these words in Matthew's Gospel trouble her. "Blessed are the poor," she says, "sounds almost mocking. Blessed are those who hunger for justice? How could that ever be?"

For Greta, the trouble with the beatitudes started in a warehouse.

The job began as just another accounting assignment to audit inventory for a client. The client was a T-shirt distributor in Kansas City, and Greta, the accountant, was present to monitor the inventory process. It was routine work, counting, checking lists, making sure the numbers lined up as they were supposed to.

So she found herself in a giant warehouse, surrounded by row upon row of T-shirts stacked to the high ceiling, boxes of T-shirts newly imported from Central America, ready to be counted and shipped to T-shirt printers and retailers across the United States.

"I looked at those T-shirts, and suddenly the room was filled with ghosts," she said. "The ghosts of the women who had made those T-shirts, sitting at sewing machines in Guatemala, El Salvador, Mexico—they were all there with me, crowding around. I could see their faces."

Indeed, Greta had met the women some months earlier, when she traveled to Mexico. Greta had started taking a few classes at Iliff School of Theology in Denver. Her class on liberation theology included a trip to Mexico to visit the people of the *maquiladoras*, the border factories where workers assemble cheap clothing for U.S. companies.

"I'm not sure what happened that day in the T-shirt warehouse, but I knew that I didn't want to stay on the treadmill of working for a bigger paycheck to buy more things—work-buy-consume, work-buy-consume. I worked for a wonderful company, a socially conscious company. We were the good guys. But I was still part of a big system that was all about the amassing of wealth. I knew those T-shirts were just one little piece of a system that kept powerful people wealthy and poor people poor. I was hungry for something more. I think I wanted something simpler.

"That was a wake-up day for me."

Not long after that warehouse awakening, Greta left her lucrative CPA career and enrolled at Iliff School of Theology. The time had come to wrestle with some vocational questions that had begun in childhood: "Growing up, I thought maybe I had a call to ministry, but it didn't seem exciting enough for me at the time. The big career in the big city seemed more glamorous."

Growing up Methodist in Aurora, Nebraska, population 4,600, Greta says she was taught to think independently and ask lots of questions. "My dad would say, 'You can go to church and hear the sermon and disagree with everything the preacher says and still be a Methodist.' It was a source of pride for us."

In Sunday school, Greta learned that something called "prophetic" ministry was a big part of her Methodist heritage, but, she says, "it was always out there and far away like a mission trip to Mexico or else it was something that happened long ago and far away, like Martin Luther King Jr. and Selma.

"I learned that racism was bad, but the only faces I ever saw in Aurora were white. I learned to appreciate what we had, but not to question why we had so much and others had so little," Greta says. "I did not question the economic structures that perpetuate poverty. I didn't know anything about that. The problems all seemed so far away."

The problems aren't so far away anymore. In her time at seminary in Denver, Greta has been able to put a face on poverty. She carries with her the faces of the maquiladora women of Mexico, and she's added the faces she's met in Denver, where she and her seminary classmates have worked with the jail chaplain, visiting inmates and hearing their stories.

"The people in jail are dehumanized," she says. "They don't have names or homes or anything. They become numbers in numbered cells. They're all in jumpsuits. Many of them are in jail waiting for their trial because they can't afford bail, or they didn't have an address to get the notice for their court date. They bounce from the street to the jail and back out to the street again. There's got to be a better way."

In search of a better way, Greta's worked with a nonprofit group called Turnabout that helps inmates find jobs when they leave jail. It's an attempt to end the bounce-back from street to jail to street again.

"There are lots of ways to look for a better way," says Greta, "and a lot of us are looking for a better way. Young people today are really waiting to be called to something."

A new Denver hip-hop band has called to Greta recently. She serves on the board of the new band Flobots and shares their unabashed advocacy for nonviolence, criminal justice reform, and peace.

"Their music is a call to wake up," says Greta, "to activate, to get involved, to be part of building justice in the world."

Flobots's website describes their music as "a fire-breathing rallying cry for all free-thinking individuals fed-up with the violence and apathy that have thus far defined the new millennium," and includes a "community" page with strong invitations to fans to "transform" themselves and their communities by engaging in neighborhood organizing, including voter registration.[1]

"I see people waking up," Greta says. "This is a time of change. This is a time of transformation."

When Greta returns home to rural Nebraska, she wants to be a pastor who wakes up people.

"I'm not called to a particular issue," she says. "I am called to be a shepherd to the comfortable flock. I see myself taking people to places like those factories in Mexico, places that bother them and disturb them and get them to see their privilege. I feel called to help people see the way things are and help them want to be part of the change.

"I have a lot of peers at school who think that people in the church don't care about justice. They think that people come to church just to socialize, just to be comfortable.

But I think that people come to church because they really want to be a part of something that matters, something that can change the world.

"And I also think they are there because they feel beaten up. Participating in this economic system is rough on everyone in different ways. The suffering of someone who works in a corporation is not the same as someone in poverty, but participating in the economic system is dehumanizing to everyone. I think we all want to be part of transformation. I'm not somebody who gets really angry when people make insensitive or unaware comments about racism or privilege. Other people are called to get angry, but I am somebody who wants to work for transformation, somebody who's hungry for justice."

Greta acknowledges that transformation is long-term work. "That's what this beatitude is saying, about hungering for justice. This is about now, about how we work for justice now, but it's also about the seeds we sow that we will not harvest ourselves. It's also true that we harvest crops we had nothing to do with sowing. This justice work is much larger than one lifetime. In this sense, we are all interconnected, the generations who went before us and the ones who will come after us.

"I think about the women who went before me and worked for women's rights," she says, "and here I am. It's still not perfect, but I've been very well supported, and I know that people went ahead of me to prepare the way for me. Likewise, I'm sure that I will work for things that I will never see come to harvest.

"Someone from the Little Rock Nine who desegregated Little Rock schools in the civil rights movement came to Iliff recently; I heard them say, 'We built bridges we will never walk across.' I believe that. In a nutshell, I think that's what this beatitude is saying: 'Blessed are the ones who build the bridges.' We're hungry for justice, and so our job is to build the bridges. I'd like to see the maquiladora workers and those inmates walk across that bridge some day," she says. "I'd like to see them walk across with names and homes and dignity."

REFLECTION

Chances are, Mick Jagger wasn't thinking of this fourth beatitude when he wrote "I can't get no satisfaction . . . 'cause I try, and I try, and I try," but the Rolling Stones rocker does touch on something of the hunger and thirst named in these words.

It's not just any hunger Jesus names with this beatitude. It's a hunger for "something more." It is the same kind of hunger that led those civil rights workers to build those bridges to equality and the same kind of hunger that led Greta Leach away from her successful financial career and into a new vocation and a new way of seeing the world. The hunger that Jesus names as blessed is the hunger for justice.

With these words, "Blessed are those who hunger and thirst for justice," Jesus again quotes the prophets.[2] This is not a call for personal or individual righteousness or moral rectitude, as some have understood from the Greek translation of this saying. It's not a call about "getting right with God." This is the prophets' call for restorative justice or distributive justice, an echo of Isaiah 61, which restores "the powerless and the outcasts to their rightful place."[3]

This kind of justice, or restoration of relationship, is something that some would call unfair. The startling new way of the kingdom Jesus announces is not about the kind of fairness we might write into our laws. This is not the justice handed down from a judge's bench, not the justice behind a policeman's badge. It is not *lex romana*, to be sure. It is not about "equal pay for equal work" or a square deal or a fair shake or any other notion we might have about fairness. This is God's alternative justice, which always pushes the ones who have the least to the head of the line. We see this kind of justice at the heart of Jesus' mission, named in the beatitudes and illustrated with the parables as Jesus announces God's desire for the world, God's passion.[4]

It is interesting that this beatitude doesn't say, "Blessed are the just" or "Blessed are those who do justice." Instead, this wisdom saying reveals that God commends the *seeking* of justice. Another saying, found later in the Sermon on the Mount, reflects this same wisdom; Jesus speaks about anxiety, telling his listeners not to worry about life, food, and clothing, and to observe the birds of the air and the lilies of the field (Matt. 6:25–33). Do not seek after food or clothing, Jesus says, but seek first God's kingdom and God's justice, and all the rest will be given. The blessing comes in the seeking, in the striving. The speaker from the Little Rock Nine echoes this beatitude with the words, "We built bridges we will never walk across." God's kingdom is not a place to reach, but rather a way to follow; God's new way is the building of those bridges to justice, not crossing over to the other side.

Sometimes this is unsettling; it doesn't seem fair. But life is not always fair. I learned that in the fifth grade. I can still see the September afternoon sun streaming in the tall, second-story windows of Miss Hilligan's fifth-grade classroom at Jefferson Elementary School. And I can see her standing beside the blackboard, erect and skinny, with short, wiry, grey-black curls and thin lips. Miss Hilligan pronounced, pursing her thin lips: "Life is not fair."

This shocked me. I had never heard this before. Nobody had ever told me that life was not fair, and all evidence up to that point, all my ten years of life, had told me that life was indeed fair. That statement, Life Is Not Fair, is the only thing I remember about the fifth grade—except for the day, later that same fall, when the principal came to the door, beckoned Miss Hilligan out into the hall, and Miss Hilligan came back into the room with tears in her eyes and said: "Children, the president has been shot. John Fitzgerald Kennedy is dead."

I've thought about Miss Hilligan many times since that autumn of 1963. I've learned that she was right. I have ample proof, as we all do, that life is not fair. We've all seen enough bad things happen to good people, enough good guys finish last, and enough bad guys at the top. But I still resist. Deep down, I want life to be fair. I want some sort of guarantee that two plus two will always equal four, that hard work gives its just rewards, that the best-laid plans will turn out as I expect, that hunger and thirst get satisfied.

But Jesus has a way of turning upside down those things we might expect. We can see this in Matthew's parable of the vineyard workers.

Jesus tells the story about a landowner who goes out to the marketplace to hire workers at six in the morning, offering them a denarius for their work, the standard wages for a day's labor. He hires more workers for the vineyard at nine, at noon, at three, and finally at five, one hour before the workday's end. At the end of the day he pays everybody one denarius whether they worked twelve hours or just one (Matt. 20:1–15).

Now, most of us would not have too much trouble seeing ourselves in that vineyard all day long, working hard, dripping with sweat, straining our back, wearing our virtue like a badge of honor. We've all been in that vineyard. We have some sense about a day's wage for a day's work. We know about what's fair and what's not. We know what it's like at work or at church or at home, somewhere we've spent a lot of time and effort; we know what it's like to give and give and give, work and work and work, hour after hour after hour, and then see somebody else—especially the new kid on the block—get all the credit, all the thanks, all the reward.

The first ones to hear this story were not so different; they knew what was fair and what was not. Most of Jesus' followers were people who found themselves at the bottom of the economic ladder, and they knew firsthand the worth of a day's work.

Matthew's community, as a new community, also understood something about being first and last. They wrestled with the status of the newcomers to their group: how would this community of Jews who were forming a new way to worship admit Gentiles into their group? They were struggling with the question of how to reconcile their differences and still care for one another and the common good. (Apparently, Matthew's community struggled a lot, because Matthew's Gospel is filled with instructions about community life, including the beatitudes, the Sermon on the Mount, several parables, and lots of pithy, riddlelike exchanges between Jesus and the disciples.) Just before presenting the parable about the vineyard workers, Matthew records an exchange between Peter and Jesus. Peter asks a question of economics: Jesus, he says, we have given up everything to follow you; what reward have you got for us? Jesus gives him not so much an answer but a riddle to ponder: the first will be last and the last first. And just after this parable, the mother of James and John, looking out for her boys' future, wants to see to it that her boys are first in line for the best seats in the house. Jesus answers that the front-row seats won't be golden thrones, but rough, hard wood shaped like a cross.

In the midst of all this instruction about what this new life with God and each other is like, comes the parable about that landowner and the vineyard workers. The story begins as expected. Jesus is describing a common practice: the landowner contracts with laborers, agreeing with them on the wage. As Jesus' listeners heard this, no doubt they nodded: that's right, a denarius equals the usual, one day's pay, subsistence pay, just enough to buy food for the worker and his family.

But the story turns at the end of the day. The landowner goes first to those most at risk. He pays the latecomers a full day's wage. They worked with no contract, no agreement, taking any work they could get before nightfall. And now they get a full day's wage, enough to feed their families. Everybody will eat tonight. The laborers who had worked since sunrise might expect twelve times as much for their full day in the vineyards. But the landowner gives those first laborers, those who agreed to work the full day for a full day's pay, exactly what he told them he would, one denarius.

The kingdom of heaven is like this, Jesus says, and it's not what we expect: the ones we might consider utterly unworthy or undeserving rank right up there at the front of the line. God's justice does not match our standards of equality. This new way of living, Jesus says, is not based upon rewards for good deeds. There is no principle of proportionality at work here, but a new kind of upside-down economics. God's economy is an economy of grace, where God showers generosity on those who might least deserve it, and at the same time God is unfailingly trustworthy to those who have nothing left to count on, nothing to hold on to at the end of the day. As Matthew's single line of interpretation (Matt. 20:16 RSV) says at the end of the parable: "So the last will be first, and the first last."

Practicing this beatitude is not easy. Not because working for justice is hard, whether finding jobs for newly released inmates or working for immigration reform. Not because building those bridges is hard work, the bridges we won't ever get to cross. Living this beatitude is not easy, I think, because it calls upon us to trust not in our good work, but only in God's extravagant and dependable grace.

For Further Reflection

1. Describe a time when you were part of "building a bridge" that you were not able to cross.
2. What do you think about the landlord in the parable (Matt. 20:1-15)? Is he just? Is he generous? In what ways?

3. Where have you found yourself as a "worker in the vineyard"? Have you been an "early hire" or a later one?

4. The early Christians struggled with the question of the status of the newcomers to their group. Name some current-day struggles with newcomers in your setting.

5. The early church wrestled with the question of diversity in community. How does your community reconcile differences and still care for one another and the common good?

6. Greta speaks of a day when the jail inmates and the border workers might "walk across with names and homes and dignity." Imagine how your community would receive such workers and former inmates.

CHAPTER FIVE

Blessed are the merciful

"Blessed are the merciful, for they
will receive mercy."—Matthew 5:7

April's story

Mercy makes us look in the mirror. That's been April Blaine's discovery as she has wrestled with these words about the merciful receiving mercy.

"Mercy goes two ways," says April. "There is something about showing mercy to others that makes you realize you need God's mercy."

April exudes competence and confidence. Words come quickly and easily to her, as she talks her way through a theological conundrum or a personal challenge. A full-time lay youth pastor and fourth-year seminary student at Methodist Theological School of Ohio, April is a sharp-witted problem solver, someone who knows how to get things done, and get them done well. She also knows that not everyone is like her.

She's learned this from her friend Laura: "I met Laura when she called the church asking for help getting milk and bread."

The day that Laura called April's church, April was eager to do the right thing, to show compassion to the stranger, to give the loaf of bread to the hungry, to love the neighbor. But she didn't know that Laura was her actual neighbor.

"I found out Laura lived about a block down the street from us," said April. "Most often, I would just refer someone like Laura to an agency, but here she was, *literally* my neighbor right here in Columbus. How could I just refer her away?

"It became personal for me. I knew that if I really claimed to want to follow this Jesus guy, I needed to do the things he says to do! Jesus says 'Love your neighbor as yourself.' So my *literal* neighbor calls and needs milk and bread, and I, who have money for milk and bread, am I going to send her to an agency? That didn't feel right. I was hit square between the eyes!"

Since that day, April and her husband have come to know their neighbor.

"Laura is always just barely getting by," says April. "She's poor, she doesn't have all of her teeth, she doesn't dress so well. And I see how people look at her, how they treat her: she doesn't get mercy, she gets judgment. They don't treat her as a person. She gets no mercy, no second chance from anybody. She never has."

Laura keeps trying to make a life for herself and her children, to establish a foothold. It's not the probability of a mission accomplished or a problem well solved that keeps April connected to Laura. April stays with Laura because she has come to know her as her neighbor.

"I hang in with Laura because I know her. I know her story. She's kind of my family now. I know her three kids. I know how much she loves her kids. Something happens when you know someone's heart and story, and you can't turn away.

"Every day she wonders if she'll be able to pay her bills and feed her kids. She frustrates me; she lives life by the seat of her pants. I want her to be more like me, to plan ahead. But I can't walk away. Sometimes I want to. I know that a lot of things she's done are her own fault. She's messed up. She's made all these mistakes. But the only way I can help her is to love her and give her space and acknowledge that she is a human being made by God.

"Laura has the ability to become whole again," said April, "and she will make mistakes again. We all do."

Laura's mistakes have made April aware of her own, as Laura's struggles have made her aware of her own advantages.

"I had a totally merciful childhood: I was loved, accepted, given the benefit of the doubt, allowed to make mistakes, and over and over again people treated me with mercy. I had very loving parents, family, teachers. I had multiple instances of people giving me grace. And then I look at Laura. Her story is just the opposite, she had none of the grace I've had, and she's suffered because of it."

Despite their differences, when April looks at Laura, she sees herself reflected back.

"The reality is: *I'm* Laura. I need mercy. I know that my tendency is to judge people, to judge someone in the first instance, to separate myself from people who aren't like me, who don't share my values or my views. I totally judge people constantly," said April, "and I judge them by the world's standards.

"The world defines us by what we do, how we behave, how we look, what we own. But God loves us just because God made us; we are children of God just *because*. The mercy and love that God shows us are not based on what we *do* but on who we *are*. It's the way a mom loves her kid; I love you because you are mine. Someone like Laura understands that. It's love not based on our actions or our ability to understand it. It's just there.

"Knowing Laura is teaching me that. Even so, I still judge others all the time."

April has also discovered that it is one thing to offer mercy to someone in obvious need like Laura, to offer compassion to the stranger, but it is quite another to offer mercy to someone who has directly hurt her. April says she's never been deeply wounded, never suffered serious harm at the hands of another, but she recounts a difficult encounter with a senior colleague that's left her questioning her ability to forgive.

"I still have a hard time forgiving him. He was the one with the power but I put myself out there, I made myself vulnerable—and I got knocked down. I feel like I was put in my place, not valued for who I was. I was dismissed. And I'm not accustomed to being dismissed."

April also ponders the distinctions between mercy and forgiveness. "Maybe I'm figuring out that mercy is when you have compassion on somebody in need, and forgiveness is what you have to offer when you've been hurt. Forgiveness is harder. Maybe forgiveness is really being able to take the next step and move on.

"I am so quick to judge my colleague and see his blind spots. I have blind spots too. For me to be compassionate, I need to take the time to hear someone's story.

"Maybe," she says, her speech slowing down, "I just need to hear his story."

Taking time to hear each other's story can change the church, April believes, and even change the world. And she has every intention of doing both:

"I am interested in reimagining the church, and I think mercy has everything to do with reimagining the church. This beatitude is about *being,* it's not about *doing.* Being church, just being church, not doing church. I am learning that we aren't very good at just being with people in their lives, in community. We want to *do* things, we want to disciple people, we want to change people, we want people to come to this program or that program. Church is so often all this stuff that people want to *do.* But people just want people to be with them, just *be* with them.

"I don't think Jesus had a five-point plan of discipleship—he just went out and loved people. I'm not saying that our programs are useless, but first we need to learn how to be with each other. I think as churches we need to look at our practices for being together, for being community—maybe that's what our programs should be about."

In a world marked by fear, suspicion, and war, April wants to see the church teach the world about love. "Our agenda, our program, our practice, should be love— healing, transformative love."

Crossing cultural, racial, economic, and national boundaries—even on a street in Columbus, Ohio—is daunting, April admits. "We don't want to mess with the others who are different. That's hard work. It takes a lot to hear somebody else's story. We don't want to do the hard work. We don't want our lives to change.

"But imagine if we became known as the people who are able to greet the other and say. '*Namaste,* the God in me greets the God in you.' Imagine if we could see ourselves in the other. We could change the world."

REFLECTION

This fifth beatitude is tricky. It seems simple enough: do mercy, get mercy. The first half matches the second half, palindrome-like, offering a sort of golden rule in the middle of the beatitudes. But it's tricky, as April Blaine discovered, because this beatitude causes us to look in the mirror.

This fifth beatitude is tricky because it can change our way of seeing. First, when we offer mercy to another, something happens that can give us a kind of rear-view vision: we begin to see the mercy that is piled up behind us already, the acts of care and kindness and forgiveness—bushel baskets of them—that have been given to us through the years. Or, second, we might offer mercy to one in need and see that looking right back at us is our own need for mercy. Or, third, a call to us for mercy can hold up a mirror that makes us want to look away, because we see reflected there our unwillingness or our inability to offer compassion. Mercy is complicated.

Maybe that's why the adjective *merciful,* the Greek *eleemon,* shows up only once in the four Gospels, only in this beatitude. Throughout the Hebrew Scriptures the word is used mostly to describe the character of God or the actions of God as God offers forgiveness to the guilty or help for those in need. Much less frequently the word is used for human beings.[1]

Nevertheless, right in the middle of the beatitudes, Jesus is saying that being merciful is blessed, commended by God, and that the merciful receive mercy. We give and we get, all in the act of compassion. And he tells more than one parable about the need for mercy, the value of compassion. These parables are the ones we know the best, the ones that have become part of the Western lexicon, the ones we assign capital letters: the Prodigal Son, the Good Samaritan. The Unforgiving Servant is Jesus' parable to instruct Peter about the need to forgive without limit—"seventy times seven" (Matt. 18:21–35 RSV). Through all these wisdom teachings, we hear again and again the one word that best describes God: compassion. And again and again the moral of the story is clear: be compassionate, be generous, be like that forgiving father with his prodigal son, be like that Samaritan who goes out of his way to help the one in the ditch. And don't be like that awful unforgiving servant, who received mercy and yet withheld it from his fellow workers. Be compassionate, as God is compassionate, be merciful as God is merciful.

But it's not so easy. Even Jesus struggled with mercy, at least once. Matthew tells the story of Jesus traveling to the coastal towns of Tyre and Sidon, where a Canaanite woman of that region approaches him and cries out: "Have mercy on me, O Lord, Son of David; my daughter is severely possessed by a demon" (15:22 RSV).

But it's Members Only.

She begs for help, Matthew records: "But [Jesus] did not answer her a word." His disciples also urge him to ignore this foreign woman, and he assures them he will not bother with her, "I was sent only to the lost sheep of the house of Israel" (15:23–24 RSV).

This woman is an outsider. She is a "triple outsider" to Jesus: she is foreign, she is a Gentile, and she is female. Three strikes against her. She is beyond the pale. And even worse, she should not even be speaking to Jesus, a Jewish male, in public. Women, foreign women no less, were never to address men in public. But her daughter is sick, and no convention is going to stop her. She comes and kneels before him and says, "Lord, help me."

Jesus answers, "It is not fair to take the children's bread and throw it to the dogs" (15:25–26 RSV).

Ouch. These aren't words we like to hear; Jesus doesn't exactly shine in this story. He refuses to heal the woman's daughter; indeed, he calls her people "dogs." This is not a portrait of the inclusive compassionate friend of the outcasts, the one who eats with tax collectors and prostitutes. Jesus is the one we expect to break social taboos, but instead we hear him uphold all the codes about shunning the one who is different. Jesus says he is not about to throw the children's food to the dogs. After all, he can hardly keep up with all the requests to heal the Jews, much less the Gentiles. And it has been a long day of jousting with the Pharisees and scribes before he ever got to Tyre and Sidon (15:1–20). There are limits to mercy, to compassion.

But she is undeterred. "Yes, Lord," she says, "yet even the dogs eat the crumbs that fall from their master's table."

"O woman," Jesus says. All of a sudden, it's as if he remembers who he is and who God is always calling him to be. The Canaanite woman has held up a mirror to Jesus. He sees that the barriers between Israel and Canaan, between Jew and Gentile, between male and female are barriers that need to come down. He sees that she is in need, and at last he says, Yes. "And her daughter [is] healed instantly" (15:27–28 RSV).

Sometimes we all, even Jesus, need a "Canaanite woman" to reflect ourselves back at us, to remind us that God's mercy, God's compassion, knows no bounds. Sometimes we need someone to help us see with fresh eyes. That's the key to practicing this beatitude: the blessing comes when we see the world with fresh eyes. How we see the world makes all the difference in how we respond to the invitation to give and receive compassion.

How we see the world matters, and, simple as it sounds, there are really only two ways to see. I learned this in seminary from Henri Nouwen. With a wave of his hand, he divided our classroom in two and said, "We stand either in the house of fear or the house of love. We see the world through the eyes of fear or the eyes of love." We see this in the parable of the good Samaritan (Luke 10:25–37).

The parable begins, as so many parables do, with a question: "What must I do to inherit eternal life?" The young lawyer wants to do the right thing. He wants to justify himself, he wants to know the rules of the game. So Jesus answers his question, in true Semitic fashion, with another question: You want life? "What is written in the law? How do you read?" (10:26 RSV).

Of course the young man knows the law. He gives the answer that is the cornerstone of the Jewish faith, the summary of the law: "Love the Lord your God with all your heart, and with all your soul, and with all your strength, and with all your mind; and your neighbor as yourself" (10:27).

But there's a question behind the lawyer's question, and though he doesn't really ask, Jesus hears it. The young lawyer wants a formula: Precisely whom must I include within my circle of neighbors, and whom may I exclude? How far do I have to stretch my love? How long? What's my job description? What are the limits of compassion?[2]

Jesus, as ever, does not deal in recipes or formulas or theories or philosophies or rules or limits, but in real life. And so he tells a story:

A man traveling down the dangerous road from Jerusalem to Jericho was robbed and stripped, beaten and abandoned for dead at the side of the road.

Down the road came a priest. He knew the temple code about the limits of good deeds. He also knew that his role was to be pure for his temple duties, and so he could not touch a dead body (and that one in the ditch looked mostly dead). He could not fulfill his obligations as priest and at the same time get mixed up with that bloodied stranger. He was a good, law-abiding person and he needed to keep his hands clean and to keep his distance, so he passed by on the other side.

Next came the Levite. He was lower in the official hierarchy than the priests, but still needing to keep ritually clean for his lesser temple duties. That man in the ditch was not his neighbor and besides, he could not take the man anywhere, he was on foot himself. He knew the codes of purity and he was a practical man. So he passed by on the other side.

And then along came a Samaritan. Now, no one hearing this story from Jesus would ever imagine that a Samaritan could be good. Good Samaritan was an oxymoron. Samaritans, every Jew knew, worshiped God in the wrong way, at the wrong place. But the Samaritan did not pass by on the other side; he came to the wounded man and Jesus says he had compassion. The Samaritan cared for the man, cleaning and bandaging his wounds, anointing them with the symbols of generosity and blessing, wine and oil, and delivering the man to an inn to recuperate.

There are two kinds of people in that story: those who see life with eyes of fear and the one who sees with eyes of love. Jesus makes it very clear to the lawyer that there is really only one rule to the game: be a neighbor. Be the one who doesn't count the cost, be the one who doesn't measure the boundaries, be the one who doesn't calculate the limits of kindness, be the one who sees.

Blessed are the merciful, the ones who see and allow themselves to be seen. As April said, "Imagine if we could see ourselves in the other. We could change the world."

For Further Reflection

1. April suggests that the church's program or agenda should be the practices of community, practices of "being together." What could such practices look like in your community?

2. April said, "We don't want to mess with the others who are different. That's hard work. It takes a lot to hear somebody else's story. We don't want to do the hard work. We don't want our lives to change." Can you describe a time when someone heard your story? Or when you heard someone else's story? What keeps us from doing this "hard work"? Why don't we want our lives to change?

3. In which character in the Good Samaritan story do you see yourself?
4. Who would be a "Samaritan," an outcast, in your community today?
5. April suggests that seeing ourselves in the other could change the world. How could this translate into national and international policies?

CHAPTER SIX

Blessed are the pure in heart

"Blessed are the pure in heart for
they shall see God."—Matthew 5:8

MARY EMILY'S STORY

"Do we really want to see God? That's my question."

Mary Emily Briehl Duba asks a lot of questions. She figures that asking questions is at the heart of the life of faith. The daughter of two Lutheran pastors, Mary Emily is not one of those PKs (pastor's kids) who grew up with the admonition to simply accept the faith of their parents, to behave well in church, and to just generally toe the line. She grew up hearing lots of questions and was encouraged to ask her own. She's still at it. Mary Emily is interested in pushing through the hard questions to discover new truths.

She grew up at Holden Village, a Lutheran retreat center her parents directed that is located in the remote Cascade Mountains of eastern Washington. "Holden sees itself as a place for the renewal of the church," Mary Emily says. "It's a place to come to for renewal, a place to explore new ideas in intentional community, a place where your boundaries get pushed a bit. People come to Holden Village because they're at a transition in their lives, and they need the space to ask the hard questions."

She loved hearing those hard questions and the exploration of new answers. Her favorite season at Holden was summertime, when summer residents and visiting scholars gathered for meals and conversations. "I spent my summer evenings sitting on our floor, listening to people talk," she says. "These were people I admired. They were awesome. They were people who were good at what they do, teachers and professors and pastors, people who cared about the church. I wanted to grow up to be a theology professor like them. They were people who practiced a kind of Christianity that to me seemed normal. They were people for whom Jesus is not just a personal savior to rescue us from the world, but rather the sign of the transformation of the world, a sign that a new way of being together as people is possible. I remember a lot of talk about imagination, about seeing new ways to do things, new ways to live together on the planet."

She remembers especially the talks about war and creative alternatives to war. "War is not inevitable; there are other ways. Imagining a new way to be in the world is critical. The words inevitable and impossible drive me crazy."

Imagining new ways to live together on the planet has stayed with Mary Emily through her college and seminary days. She is now the theologian she imagined back at Holden Village, working towards a Master of Divinity degree at Yale Divinity School, and she hopes to go on to do a Ph.D. in theology. Her focus is on ethics, with an emphasis on the Christian practices of peacemaking and nonviolence and something she calls the practice of imagination. She wants to look at how the imagination shapes identity, faith formation, and public life.

When asked what she's going to do with her academic degrees, she has a long answer about the practice of imagination, but her short answer is "cause trouble."

"Causing trouble," she says, "is at the heart of the Christian mission in the world because it's at the heart of what God's doing in the world—not trouble for trouble's sake, but trouble for transformation."

She's found ways to cause trouble throughout her college and graduate education. Her practice of peace and nonviolence has found expression in campus actions for peace and justice, leading the Peace Fellowship at Seattle University and founding the Yale Divinity School chapter of The Beatitudes Society where she's worked with her fellow seminarians on a broad range of social justice concerns. Mary Emily's "causing trouble" included a Good Friday arrest for civil disobedience at the Groton, Connecticut, nuclear submarine base; this and all of her pursuits have not been trouble for trouble's sake but have been about making the deep connection between theological conviction and public action.

This connection between the inner motivation and the outer demonstration matters to Mary Emily. Public and political action for justice is essential, she believes, but such action only has integrity if it is grounded in theological reflection. Table talk, the kind of communal conversation that she learned as a child at Holden Village, is critical:

"I'm into protesting only if it starts and ends in having soup together," she says.

The process of action and reflection gives integrity and a clarity of focus one could call "purity of heart," right?

Yet Mary Emily questions the notion of being "pure in heart."

"I'm not sure I know what that means," she is quick to say, "but I'm pretty sure I don't have a pure heart. I'm not sure I really think anybody has one."

But then she talks about Blake.

"I spent the summer after college doing in-home respite care for Blake. He was nine years old, the son of some friends from church. He has Down syndrome, palsy, microcephalia, he can't speak and is only now learning to walk.

"Caring for Blake was one of the hardest things I've ever done. I'd just gotten my philosophy degree, I was eager for graduate school, I was 'heady,' filled up with ideas. And I had this job: I would get to Blake's house everyday at 6:45 a.m. to bathe him. Fancy degrees mean nothing to him. What matters is love, and keeping the soap out of his eyes.

"We would go on smell walks. I'd pull off pine needles and lavender stalks; I'd offer them to him, and he would choose one. I'd switch the pine and the lavender back and forth in my hands, and then he'd settle on one. He would breathe it in, inhale deeply. Blake has no way of communicating, his hearing isn't good, his sight isn't good, and he has no way of reaching out to his surroundings. But with the smell walks I could watch him engage his world. And I could begin to engage the world in a new way.

"If I've ever seen God, I saw it with Blake."

Mary Emily interprets this beatitude about purity of heart as "the desire to will one thing, not to be conflicted." She experienced that with Blake.

"When I spent time with Blake that's how I felt," she says, "not conflicted. I could only be in that moment, with the lavender and the pine needles and Blake. There was no room for abstract thought.

"Even though Blake's life is limited, he has a unique ministry in our community," she says. "He is a window into the heart of God. When I'm with him, I'm in the presence of Life—the kind of life that overcomes death, the kind of life that casts out words like 'inevitable' and 'impossible,' the kind of life that transforms the world.

"That's when you can recognize God. That's when you can see God. In that moment, you can see how life is overcoming death, transforming the world.

"That doesn't mean it is easy. It's so hard. I'd go home after six hours with Blake and I would need to think and talk about something else. It's so intense."

In light of her experience with Blake, the sixth beatitude, "Blessed are the pure in heart for they will see God," is a challenge.

"We assume that seeing God is something we want," Mary Emily says, "but I'm not so sure. We live so that we won't see God. We avoid the places where God is visible, those little windows into the heart of God—the lives of the poor, the beauty and brokenness of creation, the margins of society.

"We think we don't have time for people like Blake because they challenge our perception of ourselves, of God, and of the world. I had to learn to slow down, to rediscover my own worth outside of my academic accomplishments, to judge others not by what they can do or produce, but by who they are as children of God.

"Accepting these challenges can be scary. We're afraid of what seeing God will do to us. Will we have to give up an easy life? Our version of success? Will we be changed? Will we ever be able to go back to the way we were?" Mary Emily's questions don't stop.

"Do we really want transformation?" she asks. "That's my big question. Do we really want to see God?"

REFLECTION

Mary Emily Briehl Duba's big question is a good one—
"Do we really want to see God?" And this beatitude is a
daunting one, or at least it has been portrayed as daunting
by too many theologians who treat "pure in heart" as
some kind of achievement to reach on the steep upward
ladder toward God.

This beatitude makes me think of the Lutheran liturgy
of my childhood, singing those phrases from Psalm 51:
"Create in me a clean heart, O God, and renew a right
spirit within me." I wasn't sure what those words meant,
but it sounded hard and holy, like some feat I couldn't
quite manage. I figured that singing those lines from the
hymnal would clean my heart, and so I sang them right
on tune, as if my life depended on it. (I must have missed
the pastor's preaching about grace.)

 To be pure of heart has nothing to do with achievement. It has nothing to do with the ancient Hebrew purity
codes about ritual cleanliness or any codes of behavior or
pathways to perfection we may have devised since that
time. Purity of heart is simply about matching our outsides
with our insides, our actions with our intentions. As a
friend of mine said, it's about the journey of becoming
our true selves. Another word for this is *integrity*.

For the ones who first heard this saying of Jesus, the
word "heart" meant much more than the cardiac muscle
that pumps our life blood. The heart was the center of the
human person, the seat of feeling and thinking and acting, the source of one's conduct. In first-century Palestine,
purity of heart meant the same thing it means today to
Mary Emily: "to will one thing, not to be conflicted."[1]

This kind of purity is rooted in what Glen Stassen calls biblical realism rather than Greek idealism. This is his salient point about all of the beatitudes: these sayings of Jesus are not meant to be hurdles to cross on the way to perfection or personal righteousness. Instead, the beatitudes are Jesus' way to point to the presence of God in our world. If indeed one wants to imagine a ladder, God has "descended" such a ladder and arrived in our midst, available in the places in our world where we encounter the poor in spirit, the mourning, the meek, and all the rest. The beatitudes, and indeed the Christian life, are not about accomplishment but rather acceptance of the great grace of a God who meets us in those places of poverty, mourning, humility, mercy, justice seeking, peacemaking, and integrity.[2]

Although later Christian teaching interpreted this beatitude as a commendation for ascetic practice to purify "evil desires,"[3] Matthew makes clear throughout his entire collection of Jesus' teaching that purity of heart is the integration of interior motive and outward action. In the later sayings of the Sermon on the Mount, Matthew includes Jesus' instruction about integrity in the practice of prayer (6:1-34), about one's treasure revealing one's heart (6:19-21), and about the eye revealing the inner self (6:22-23). Throughout Matthew's Gospel and the other Gospel versions of the Jesus story, we hear Jesus call for hearts that are focused on God and actions that care for God's world. A heart so focused is an undivided heart, a pure heart, that "wills one thing," and that "one thing" is the new kingdom of God announced by Jesus, a kingdom marked by God's generous love and compassion for all.

Jesus' followers knew that his teaching about purity was not the same as the temple's teaching about purity. In fact, Jesus defied the holiness codes with a continued series of teaching and action that raised the ire of the religious authorities. I can imagine Jesus saying these words with an emphasis on *heart*, ("Blessed are the pure in *heart*") making the point that purity of heart matters more than dietary rules or practices, as he says in Matthew 15: "It is not what goes into the mouth that defiles a person, but it is what comes out of the mouth that defiles . . . to eat with unwashed hands does not defile" (vv. 11, 20).

Jesus' followers also knew that his teaching was not limited to their personal integrity or personal practices. This call for purity of heart is—like all the beatitudes—a call for an alternative kind of social vision and practice, a new way to order community life. This was a call for a new kind of politics, as Marcus Borg names it in *Meeting Jesus Again for the First Time*, the "politics of compassion" as opposed to the "politics of purity." The purity codes determined much more than temple practices; they determined the politics, that is, the social practices of the entire community. Purity laws dictated social ranking, defining the elite and the outcast, naming who was "whole" and who was not, and determining who could eat with whom. These purity codes determined much about not only religious life but economic well-being, creating a culture marked by distinct social and economic boundaries. As Borg succinctly put it, "Whereas purity divides and excludes, compassion unites and includes."[4]

Jesus' alternative way in both word and deed defied the purity system. The Gospels give us multiple examples of Jesus crossing barriers and breaking taboos in order to include the "unclean" ones at the margins: healing on the Sabbath, dining with the tax collectors and prostitutes, speaking to women in public, speaking with foreign women, healing Gentiles, including women as his disciples, and offering parables about a "good" Samaritan or a banquet table filled with social outcasts. With his deeds and words, Jesus showed that God is not concerned with a system of boundaries and taboos but rather with the ones who need help: God is a God not of rules, but of compassion.

This beatitude, like all the others, is an invitation to an alternative vision, a vision and a way of life that was not the dominant norm of Jesus' day. The invitation to be pure in heart is an invitation to participate in the compassion of God, and so to see God.

Matthew invites us to this alternative way to "see God" with a story that illustrates the beatitudes and challenges the "politics of purity." In Matthew 25 we hear the dramatic story of a "last judgment." This is the Matthew of gnashing teeth and end-of-time absolutes. Matthew's language in this passage is the language of his tradition, words about insiders and outcasts—not the language of the beatitudes, but words that his community would recognize. Matthew writes about the separation of the sheep and the goats: the insiders were the sheep, the members of the flock, and the outsiders were the goats. Insiders were those who followed the teachings of the temple, the outsiders were everybody else. But for all the traditional language here, for all the words that rang familiar, these words were shocking.

The surprise for Matthew's listeners was not the business of end-time judgment. That concept had been part of Judaism for several centuries already. From ancient times, they had codified a system of everlasting reward and punishment into institutional religion; the "politics of purity" was intended to guarantee a good and righteous life with God now and forever. Into this system come the words of Jesus, the new "politics of compassion." Using the familiar images of sheep and goats, the familiar concept of reward and punishment from the prophet Ezekiel, Matthew turns it around and upside down: You want reward and punishment? Let me show you reward and punishment. Let me show you insiders and outsiders. Let me show you what really matters. The key to life, the key to a pure heart, the key to seeing God, Jesus says, is not religious observance, but how we care for each other. To be with God, forever and ever, for time eternal and right now, is to care for one another. We give the cup of cold water not in order to enter some heavenly gates somewhere when we die, but to touch God here and now, because God has already touched us.

While Jesus' words reflect the ancient prophets' teaching about neighbor love, there is something new here. Jesus says that in meeting the one in need, we meet divinity. Something more than a cup of water or a piece of bread changes hands: "As you did it to the least of these . . . you did it to me" (Matt. 25:40 RSV). We find that when we give the cup, share the bread, we encounter the presence of God in that person in need. We see God. How can that be?

When we give that cup of water or visit that one in need or welcome that one who is outside, the shape of our heart changes, the boundaries of our hearts ease. The encounter with the one in need calls on the depths of our own strength and at the same time highlights our own weakness. We might want to look away, to avoid the illness or hunger or pain or loss we see in the other. One person's singular ordeal or the reality of global poverty can overwhelm us. But when we look to that other and recognize something of ourselves and our own place of need, our own desire for God's healing, we can glimpse that "window into the heart of God." It is not a simple cause and effect, doing good and so finding God, doing love and so feeling love, or vice versa. It is a process of transformation at the core of our being that cannot take place apart from the kind of active love—compassion— that Matthew describes. As we are transformed, we participate in the compassion of God. "As you did it to the least of these you did it to me."

With our new focus, with purity of heart, Matthew's apocalyptic stage props—the judgment throne, the saved sheep and damned goats, the system of rewards and punishments—give way to the real images Jesus named, which begin to take shape in our world in ways both personal and corporate: "I was hungry" becomes a bag of groceries at the local food pantry and also a national farm bill; "I was thirsty" becomes emergency relief to flood victims and also long-term water pollution control; "I was a stranger" becomes a welcome to the newcomer in the pew and also federal immigration reform; "I was naked" becomes a supply of winter coats at the shelter and also fair wages for textile workers; "I was sick" becomes oil anointing the forehead of a cancer patient and also uni-versal health care; "I was in prison" becomes a visit to an inmate and also an end to torture in American prisons. "As you did it to the least of these you did it to me."

In the place of human need, we see the Life that Mary Emily described as "the kind of life that overcomes death, the kind of life that casts out words like 'inevitable' and 'impossible,' the kind of life that transforms the world." We see God.

FOR FURTHER REFLECTION

1. "Causing trouble is at the heart of the Christian mission," said Mary Emily. What Christian trouble-makers can you name? Have you ever caused trouble in this sense, "trouble for transformation"?

2. Mary Emily said, "I'm into protesting only if it starts and ends in having soup together." Describe a similar kind of reflection exercise that you have experienced. What kind of reflection-practice process could you begin in your community?

3. Can you describe past (or present) experiences when you have felt that Christianity is about achievement?

4. Can you give examples of the "politics of purity," codes for acceptable and unacceptable behavior that exist today? How might the "politics of compassion" make a difference?

CHAPTER SEVEN

Blessed are the peacemakers

"Blessed are the peacemakers, for they
will be called children of God."—Matthew 5:9

KENT'S STORY

Born in Saigon at the height of the Vietnam War, Kent
Sensenig was born—quite literally—a peacemaker. His
Mennonite missionary parents had traveled from Lancaster County, Pennsylvania, to South Vietnam in the
1960s to take a tangible stand for nonviolence in the
face of the war. Working with other Mennonites, the
Sensenigs ran a community center and founded the first
Vietnamese Mennonite congregation. They also joined
in periodic relief efforts to war victims, especially during the Tet Offensive of 1968, when the war came right
into the city.

When the family left Vietnam to return to Lancaster
County, they didn't leave the war behind. Kent's father
continued his work with the Mennonites, working on
refugee resettlement. Questions about the war and peacemaking were daily dinner-table fare.

"The war stretched Mennonites to think about our
response," Kent says. "Was it enough to provide relief
to the victims of war? Was it enough to register as a con-
scientious objector, to separate ourselves from the war?
Should we not rather be speaking up to prevent war in
the first place?"

Such questions have stayed with Kent and continue to shape his daily life and work. He enrolled at Fuller Theological Seminary in Pasadena, California, to study the theology of peacemaking, attracted in particular to ethicist Glen Stassen's work on "just peacemaking."

"I'm interested in building bridges between just war theory and the pacifist tradition. I come from my Anabaptist-Mennonite tradition, my strong tradition that says no to war. I accept that no. But now, how do we go further than that and say yes to peace?"

Getting at answers to that question has shaped Kent's doctoral studies and his very lifestyle. His dissertation is about the relationship between land and theology, as seen in three periods of history: first-century Galilee, seventeenth-century England, and twentieth-century Kentucky.

"I believe that place shapes you. I'm looking at Jesus as a Galilean, and Galilee as a region that shaped Jesus. And I'm studying two groups of English Baptists, the Diggers and the Levellers, who were devoted to the antiprivatization of the commons. And I'm looking at Wendell Berry, a Southern Baptist, and his place-based theology, his strong commitment to sustainable economics and democracy." He laughs an easy, relaxed laugh: "I'm tracing radical Christian politics."

Saying yes to peace involves more than opposition to war, he says. "We need to begin by making peace with the creation. We need to conserve our resources, to use them in a way that is sustainable. We need to start right where we live."

For Kent and his wife, Jennifer Davis Sensenig, a Mennonite pastor, "starting where they live" has brought them in close contact with the land, from the concrete sidewalks of Pasadena to the farmlands of the Midwest. At Fuller Seminary, they buck the Southern California devotion to the private automobile and do not own a car. "It keeps your life more local," Kent says.

Farming has been a significant part of their commitment to peacemaking. They are strong advocates of Community Supported Agriculture (CSA)[1] and Kent has also spent several seasons working on farms that grow food for subscribing families.

"I have worked on CSA farms and gardens for eleven seasons—it's kind of a perennial 'summer job,'" he chuckles. "I ran my own CSA garden in Iowa for three years called One Iowa Acre with twenty to twenty-five 'shareholder' member households, the core group of which was members of our Mennonite church in town."

Whether musing about the goodness of locally produced groceries or comparing John Howard Yoder's pacifism to Reinhold Niebuhr's Christian realism, Kent speaks not with a zealot's intensity but rather with a farmer's unhurried cadence. He speaks like someone who knows where he belongs. And his words always return to his roots in a family of peacemakers.

"My family narrative is about peace. I heard from my earliest days that peacemaking is at the heart of the gospel. I heard that peacemakers belong to God. Peacemakers are the children of God. That's powerful, evocative language," he says. "That's deeper than anything, deeper than any creed, to know yourself to be a child of God. That identity is a source of power.

"Once you understand that you are a child of God," he says, "you recognize that all people are brothers and sisters, we're all siblings. Out of that comes the dynamic of breaking down barriers. You see that there are no barriers. The peacemakers who are the most powerful and effective sense this; they know themselves to be beloved of God, as Jesus knew himself to be beloved, a child of God. That was at the heart of Jesus' spirit, that source of love and affirmation."

Despite Kent's own easy manner, he acknowledges that this identity of being a child of God, a peacemaker, is far from easy. "This practice of following Jesus as a peacemaker shapes our vocations, our lives. It's not about having lives that might look successful. It can lead to some struggles. It's counter-intuitive to receive the blessing of being a peacemaker. It means doing crazy things like going to Vietnam in the 1960s or living on a farm in the twenty-first century."

Being a peacemaker does not mean attempting to rise to some impossible standard, in Kent's view. It means responding to God's invitation to transformation.

"God is inviting us to participate, to make peace with creation," Kent says. "That's what's at the heart of the gospel. We are in such intimate relationship with other beings. In the Genesis story, God calls us to give names to all creatures, to give honor in the naming, and this naming binds us in intimate relationship with all creation. We are called to tend the garden."

God's invitation to transformation can be seen throughout the Bible, he says, in the way that the biblical story "arises out of a backdrop of empire.

"A good way to read the Bible," he says, "is to see it as a series of counter-empire initiatives undertaken by God. Abraham leaves civilization's center in Mesopotamia and heads out for the periphery of Canaan; he turned away from the first great conquest state; he left that to answer God's call. The Hebrew people are birthed—in one sense literally, by the civilly disobedient midwives Shiphah and Puah who save the baby Moses from the murderous Pharaoh—in the shadow of the hubristic pyramids of Egypt, as a slave revolt from the other great empire of the ancient Near East. And Jesus himself comes into the world a few short years after the elevation of the greatest emperor the world had ever seen, Caesar Augustus. Jesus is counter to the Empire.

"My general view," he says, "is that God does not desire God's creation or creatures to be dominated by empires."

Kent's own response to God's invitation to transformation is based on the life of Jesus. "The place for me to start and end is Jesus. I want to translate creatively from the first century to our own, to take practical steps. What did Jesus do?"

In answer to this, Kent has compiled "The Top Fourteen Spiritual-Political Practices of Jesus," a list that includes prophetic actions (that he names as street theater, civil disobedience, and social activism such as the donkey ride into Jerusalem, overturning temple tables, and breaking Sabbath laws); subversive storytelling of parables that turned the world upside-down and redefined "reality"; feeding the hungry; forgiving debts; sharing wealth; eating with outcasts; being a "radical feminist" of the first century by befriending and advocating for women and children and by empowering the Samaritan woman to be the first evangelist and Mary Magdalene to be the first apostle; and contemplative prayer.

Kent's translation of Jesus' "spiritual-political practices" ranges from local food to barrier-breaking interfaith dialogue. "I'm interested in grassroots peacemaking, in the practical things we can do: simple living, local food, microcredit banks, not being car dependent, crossing barriers, talking with folks from other religious traditions. Peacemaking is not just about war versus peace, it pervades every choice we make, every conversation we might have."

The steps to peacemaking may be grassroots but they cannot be limited to individuals. They are something for the community to participate in, Kent says, something for local churches to place at the center of their worship life. "Peacemaking is not optional, not a secondary program for the church. It's about cooperating in a sustainable way in this age of ecological meltdown. The fundamental task for our generation is to draw on the peacemaking tradition of the Bible and transform the way we live."

Reflection

Seven words give us just about everything we need to know about practicing this beatitude, seven words from a twentieth-century pope: "If you want peace, work for justice." With these words, Paul VI in 1972 named the origin of Jesus' teaching about peace, the Jewish concept of shalom: peace is not simply the absence of war, but the well-being of the people, as described by the prophet Isaiah's "swords into plowshares" and Micah's words "They shall all sit under their own vines and under their own fig trees, and no one shall make them afraid" (Isa. 2:4; Mic. 4:4).

It's taken me decades to learn this. I used to think that peacemaking simply meant ending war. As one who came of age in the Vietnam War, with my two brothers watching their draft lottery numbers, staying in school to avoid the draft, and ultimately getting drafted and serving in the National Guard, the war and the body count on the evening news was front and center in my family's daily life. My heroes were Daniel and Philip Berrigan, with their dramatic protests against the war. I saw peacemaking as stopping that war: "Blessed are the peacemakers" meant "Blessed are the war protesters." A decade or so later, with Vietnam over, the Cold War was heating up with the massive weapons buildup of the early 1980s. I was working for an interfaith nuclear disarmament group,[2] and I saw peacemaking as ending the nuclear arms race: "Blessed are the weapons protesters."

But a rabbi's question helped me see that peacemaking is something more. I went to talk with Rabbi Leonard Beerman[3] one day in the early 1980s when I was discouraged, feeling that it was futile to protest the nuclear arms race when the nuclear stockpiles rose higher each day and the weapons budgets swelled bigger each day, and every day our country sold more and more weapons to more and more eonomically undeveloped countries. "Our efforts are so puny and nobody cares, nobody listens, nobody can change anything. Why do we bother to keep working for social and political change?" I asked him.

Rabbi Beerman listened, as he always listened to my questions and complaints, and in his gentle, quiet way reached into his desk and brought out a picture of his new grandson, Matthew Benjamin. He asked to see a picture of my new baby son, Benjamin Michael. He told me to think about these two little boys who would graduate from high school in the year 2000. He told me to think about what we owed them. And then he asked me, "If we cannot cultivate a passion for what one human being owes to another, what are we?"]

From that rabbi, and that question, I began to learn about shalom, about what we human beings owe to one another as children of God. I began to develop a passion not just for ending war, but also for seeking justice. I began to understand those words of Pope Paul VI and Micah. My own focus shifted from arguing about the potential devastation of a nuclear war to the growing devastation of a militarized global economy. As President Dwight Eisenhower had said back in 1953, "Every gun that is made, every warship launched, every rocket fired signifies, in the final sense, a theft from those who hunger and are not fed, those who are cold and are not clothed. This world in arms is not spending money alone. It is spending the sweat of its laborers, the genius of its scientists, the hopes of its children."[4]

While it's taken me a few decades to learn about peacemaking, it's also taken the Christian church a few centuries. Since the armies of Constantine first marched under the banner of the Christian cross, Christians have made ethical arguments for and against war based on either pacifism or "just war" theory. (There was also the regrettable period of the crusades of the Middle Ages, when holy war against "infidels" was justified and sanctioned by the church; that position is no longer considered justifiable!) Christian pacifists have maintained a tradition for nonviolent resistance to war since the time of Jesus, basing pacifism on a variety of biblical texts including the fifth commandment against murder, this seventh beatitude, and Jesus' teaching in the Sermon on the Mount to turn the other cheek (Matt. 5:39). Just war theory, codified for the church by St. Augustine at the beginning of the fifth century, has been an attempt to answer the question, "When, if ever, is it justifiable for a Christian to participate in war?" The tenets of just war say that war can only be waged (1) as a last resort, (2) by a legitimate authority, (3) to redress a grievous wrong, (4) with reasonable assurance of success, (5) to establish peace, (6) with violence proportional to the injury suffered, and (7) with weapons that discriminate between combatants and civilians. With the dawn of modern warfare, these tenets have often been breached, to say the least.

We now have a new paradigm for peacemaking that is changing the conversation about war and peace. It is called "just peacemaking" and seeks to address the complexities of a world marked by terrorism, nuclear weapons, unchecked ethnic genocide, and nearly perpetual war. Rather than focusing on the question of war—whether to resist or to wage it—just peacemaking asks a new question entirely. The argument, as named in Glen Stassen's 1992 book *Just Peacemaking: Transforming Initiatives for Justice and Peace,*[5] moves from "Should we go to war?" or "Should we go to this war?" to "How can we *prevent* war?" In answer to that last question, just peacemaking offers more than a third ethical theory. Just peacemaking gives us initiatives that can prevent war and build the conditions for peace.

We can see such peacemaking initiatives in the Sermon on the Mount. Stassen calls them "transforming initiatives," teachings offered by Jesus to diagnose and break the cycles of violence and introduce God's new way of peace and reconciliation. Stassen argues that these teachings that illustrate the beatitudes are not so-called hard sayings or high ideals merely meant to oppose the traditional teachings, but are instead a way of deliverance from the vicious cycles of anger, domination, and violence.[6]

It works like this: first, Jesus names the traditional teaching, such as "You shall not kill" (Matt. 5:21); second, he diagnoses the vicious cycles that lead to violence and murder, "anger" (Matt. 5:22); and third, he offers release with a new and unexpected behavior, a transforming initiative, "be reconciled"(Matt. 5:23-26). Rather than setting the bar even higher with a command such as "do not be angry," Jesus offers a way out of anger: go to your brother, be reconciled. (I hear these words and picture my son's soft-voiced kindergarten teacher saying "Use your words, children.") The transforming initiative, says Stassen "moves from the powerlessness of being stuck in anger toward the empowerment of participating in God's way of grace and new life."[7]

When Jesus names the traditional revenge cycle of "an eye for an eye" in the Sermon on the Mount (Matt. 5:38) he does not simply offer the opposite alternative, "Do not seek revenge," but instead invites a third way, a new behavior: "Turn the other cheek" (Matt. 5:39). This proactive initiative interrupts the expected cycle of behavior and offers a surprising alternative that can transform the situation. We see this again in Jesus' teaching about loving enemies (Matt. 5:43–45): the tradition that he addresses is exclusive love for our neighbors and hatred for our enemies (the expected purity codes), but Jesus says that such love is too easy. He invites us to go outside the boundaries of tribalism or nationalism and get to know and love our enemies. Only then are we transformed, and the cycle of violence has the possibility of being broken.[8]

Just peacemaking theory is more than theory. A broad-based group of twenty-three scholars have worked with Stassen's just peacemaking theory and developed ten tangible and proven practices for preventing war: "Just peacemaking theory seeks to be realistic in the sense that it focuses on what in fact works to prevent wars in real history, based on empirical reality."[9] The ten practices, all of which have been "tested in the field" around the globe in international and neighborhood conflicts, include cooperative conflict resolution (used in the former Yugoslavia as well as with United States urban street gangs); sustainable economic development (such as microbanking, local industries, and sustainable farming); and nonviolent direct action (as seen in the Indian independence movement led by Gandhi or the American civil rights work of Martin Luther King, Jr.)[10]

Kent Sensenig's local and daily practices spring from his embrace of these strategies. These are the strategies of shalom, the strategies for creating the world that Micah and Isaiah envisioned. These are the strategies that we need in order to practice this beatitude. And these are the strategies that invite us into relationship not only with our "enemies," but also with God. The peacemakers, Jesus tells us, are the "children of God."

To be recognized as children of God, as Kent said, is a source of empowerment: "That's deeper than anything, deeper than any creed, to know yourself to be a child of God. . . . Once you understand that you are a child of God, you recognize that all people are brothers and sisters, we're all siblings. Out of that comes the dynamic of breaking down barriers. You see that there are no barriers. The peacemakers who are the most powerful and effective sense this; they know themselves to be beloved of God, as Jesus knew himself to be beloved, a child of God. That was at the heart of Jesus' spirit, that source of love and affirmation."

We can see this recognition of a shared humanity in the postapartheid work of Archbishop Desmond Tutu and South Africa's Truth and Reconciliation Commission. "Our nation sought to rehabilitate and affirm the dignity and personhood of those who for so long had been silenced, had been turned into anonymous, marginalized ones," wrote Tutu in his book *No Future without Forgiveness*. "Now they would be able to tell their stories, they would remember, and in remembering would be acknowledged to be persons with an inalienable personhood." South Africa made a strategic and unprecedented decision—a just peacemaking initiative—to redress the wrongs of apartheid not with Nuremburg-style trials nor with blanket amnesty or "national amnesia," but with an acknowledgment of relationship, a "third way," granting amnesty to individuals in exchange for a full disclosure of their crimes.[11]

This third way, Tutu said, arose from the African understanding of the common bond between all people, *ubuntu*: "Ubuntu is very difficult to render into a Western language," he wrote. "It speaks of the very essence of being human . . . it is to say 'my humanity is caught up, inextricably bound up, in yours.' We belong in a bundle of life. We say, 'a person is a person through other persons.'. . . A person with *ubuntu* . . . has a proper self-assurance that comes from knowing that he or she belongs in a great whole and is diminished when others are humiliated or diminished, when others are tortured or oppressed, or treated as if they were less than who they are."[12]

Living this seventh beatitude is not a one-size-fits-all proposition. Sometimes we are called to be war protesters; sometimes we are called to be weapons protesters; some of us are called to be pacifist war resisters, and some of us might be called to war. But all of us, always, are invited to remember that we "belong in a bundle of life." All of us, always, need to keep asking the rabbi's question: "If we cannot cultivate a passion for what one human being owes to another, what are we?" And all of us, always, are children of God who want peace, and so, as the pope says, we work for justice: "Blessed are the just peacemakers."

FOR FURTHER REFLECTION

1. Kent said his "family narrative is about peace." How would you describe your family narrative?
2. Kent said, "God does not desire God's creation or creatures to be dominated by empires," and "Jesus is counter to the Empire." What evidence of dominating empire might Jesus counter today, in our world?
3. Name some grassroots peacemaking initiatives that your small group—or church or community—might start. What might you do at home?
4. Describe a time when you have been a war protester or a weapons protester, a pacifist or one who served in war. What role did this beatitude play for you at that time?

5. What does the rabbi's question mean to you?
6. Name a conflict in your experience that could use a just peacemaking initiative. How might you begin?

CHAPTER EIGHT

Blessed are those who are persecuted for justice's sake

"Blessed are those who are persecuted for justice's sake, for theirs is the kingdom of heaven."
—Matthew 5:10

JEREMY'S STORY

"There's so much danger in it."

Jeremy Scott does not look like a man who would court danger, but the juxtaposition of the words blessed and persecuted in this beatitude spell danger for him in a way that calls to him, unsettles him, and is changing his life.

Warm, generous, pleasant, affable, mild-mannered, even—these are all words that come to mind upon meeting Jeremy. He has no apparent hard edges. But he is sharp about his perception of his place in a world marked by injustice, oppression, and persecution.

"There's so much danger in this beatitude. It's so easy for us to impose ourselves, to think we are persecuted. I hear it in my student colleagues who call it 'persecution' when their cherished long-held views get challenged with new ways of thinking. That's uncomfortable, but that's not persecution. That's seminary.

"I have no idea what it is to be truly persecuted! I likely never will. We are the persecutors in ways we never understand, because of our privilege. What's dangerous is that we don't see our privilege," Jeremy says. "My social location keeps me safer than about 80 percent of humanity. I'm blond, blue-eyed, white, middle class, male, educated. I can't undo any of that. I have a built-in support network; I'm three phone calls away from help at any time. I epitomize privilege.

"I've had a hard time coming to peace with that."

Whatever peace Jeremy has reached is neither a quiet complacency nor a retreat into thanksgiving for the blessings and benefits of privilege, but rather a profound theological shift that causes him to ask hard questions about what he calls the "inherited assumptions" of his faith and his own vocation as a pastor.

Jeremy is a student at Methodist Theological School in Ohio, and he lives on the serene campus just outside Columbus with his wife and young son. Before coming to seminary, he was a top-salaried software engineer. He was living the proverbial good life, but living, he said "someone else's expectations."

"I had money, authority, discretion. We had a new son. I had it all. But something was missing. I wasn't where I was supposed to be."

Not unlike many of his colleagues at seminaries and divinity schools across the nation, Jeremy came to seminary in search of "something more."

He's found it. In fact he's found more, much more, than he expected. He's been able to wrestle with some of those "inherited assumptions" of the faith, some of the pat answers to hard questions. And he's discovered a vocation he didn't know he had, a vocation to pay attention and call attention to those who suffer.

Jeremy's childhood gave him the lenses with which to discover his place in the world: "I guess you could say that I was at the picked-on end of the spectrum in junior high. I was socially awkward, like most young boys. My father died in a boating accident when I was six years old so I grew up never really understanding what boys are supposed to be like, act like. Being overweight, being from not the most affluent family, nothing about me was admirable to my peers; it's always easy to pick on the big kid. I was on the outside.

"My grandparents were every-Sunday Christians and they brought me to church. I discovered that church was the only place that I could be more myself, a place where I was affirmed. Older adults there took an interest in me, as a person, a good person. I didn't know it at the time, but I was experiencing God in those people. I belonged. I wasn't on the outside anymore."

Jeremy describes his own experience of childhood, at the picked-on end of the spectrum, as the mildest form of persecution: "My own experience wasn't so bad, but maybe it helped me get some idea of what it's like for others. We all have a choice to identify with others or not, to try to see their place in the world or not. We are all blessed and burdened with this ability to choose."

Jeremy chooses to see life from the margins, from the place of the one who is hurting.

Some of this begins in his own hurt, as a six-year-old boy losing his father, as a college freshman losing his best friend to death. At a too-early age, Jeremy began to deal with the great theological question of theodicy, the question of evil: why do bad things happen to good people?

"God doesn't cause evil, but God created a world that makes evil possible," Jeremy figures. "God doesn't keep us in a bubble. I think about how much I have to protect my son. But I have to let him grow up and make his own choices. Love allows that."

Jeremy works hard to explain his newfound understanding of God's love that challenges some childhood notions of God as all-powerful: "God did not create us and the world as puppets for God to control. Instead God created us to be in relation with God as I am in relation with other people and animals, or as I am in my relationship to my son. I exert control over him in that I shape his world in some degree, but I don't pull his strings and make him do exactly as I want.

"So I cannot blame God for not pulling strings to magically make things better just as I cannot blame my toaster for not making coffee. It simply isn't in the nature of God for it to work that way."

The presence of evil in the world is not part of some divine plan, Jeremy asserts, but rather the result of human greed. And one evil in particular has caught Jeremy's attention: modern-day slavery.

When Jeremy hears "Blessed are the persecuted" he thinks of the stories he knows about young girls and boys sold by their unwitting and impoverished families into lives of unimaginable cruelty.

"I don't think you get much more persecuted than that: someone takes your freedom, your body, your personality, your family, all those things God gifts us with, our very humanity, and then imposes things, strips you of your personhood. What could be more extreme than having every moment controlled by another for the benefit of the other, controlled by fear, coercion, robbed even of mental escape? It's physical persecution but it's also emotional persecution; that's so much more lasting."

Jeremy first discovered modern-day slavery when looking on The Beatitudes Society website for a project for his campus chapter of The Beatitudes Society. He saw that author Dave Batstone was speaking on campuses about his campaign to end the global slave trade.

"I thought 'slave trade'? You've got to be kidding me. So I ordered the book and spent the next two weeks reading it. I hated the book. I spent two weeks hating the book. But I couldn't stop reading it."

Jeremy says that he couldn't stop reading because of his son. "It probably sounds a little oxymoronic, but having him has made everything personal in a way that's not about me."

With more slaves in bondage today than at any time in history—twenty-seven million—and at least half of them children, Jeremy wants people to know that slavery exists in restaurant kitchens and brothels in the heartland of our country. In front of our eyes and yet invisible, the slave trade is plied "on Main Street, USA," and Jeremy wants us to pay attention.

Jeremy has become one of the new twenty-first century abolitionists. He decided to invite author Batstone to his campus, and the idea blossomed into a day-long conference called Liberation!, attracting participants from all around Columbus and throughout the state. "We had evangelical pastors and mainline pastors, Catholic nuns, a retired bishop, social service providers, nurses, people from OSU law school. We had conservatives and liberals and Democrats and Republicans and the whole nine yards!"

He's now taken on a new volunteer role, in addition to his seminary work, to become State Director of the

Ohio Not for Sale Campaign. There are many aspects to this kind of work, from participating in the new "underground railroad" that coordinates the new abolitionists across the globe who are rescuing the victims of the global slave trade, to staging local educational events for schools, churches, and community groups. But it's the root cause of slavery that gets Jeremy.

"Families in good economic condition don't sell their daughters. If a family has a decent source of income, they don't sell their daughters. I'm interested in addressing the poverty that produces slavery. That's my passion."

And this means change in our own habits, he says, change that many won't welcome: "When you are paying four dollars for a T-shirt, you are helping to support slavery. We know that sweatshop labor predisposes people to trafficking. We need to use America's economic power to say no to the import of sweatshop goods.

"We as a country need to decide that we're not going play on that field. We need to elevate the playing field for everybody. We need to raise the standard for everybody."

Elevating the playing field means support of microlending opportunities as well as support of national legislation that blocks the import of goods produced in exploitative conditions.

"We have already set up barriers to prevent the import of clothing trimmed in cat and dog fur," he says, "because of outrage over the abuse of animals. Now we realize we need to protect human beings as well as dogs and cats."

The connection between persecution and blessing in this beatitude is a complicated one. Slaves are not "persecuted for justice" in the sense that martyrs have been persecuted; they are far from willing victims of their suffering. And while some might see some sort of equation between those who suffer and the blessings in store for them, Jeremy has no time for that: "There's a tendency to romanticize those who suffer: we say 'Look how much closer this suffering is bringing you to God'—that is *so* abusive!"

Instead, he holds that the persecuted, especially the poorest of the poor who are invisible laborers in unjust globalized economic structures, offer us a new way to see reality: "I don't think anyone but those who live in real persecution can truly speak to these things, but I can say that the deeply persecuted offer a mirror to the rest of us, or, as Jon Sobrino put it, 'A light whose power is capable of unmasking lies is very beneficial and very necessary. This is the light offered by the crucified people.'"[1]

Jeremy is willing to look into the mirror and see the light. "I look at senseless deaths—my father, my best friend, just last year my godson, and two days later my son's godfather—and I say that there was nothing I could have done to stop those deaths. Nothing anybody could have done. So I take from that a sense of duty to do something about the deaths I can prevent: the death of a twelve-year-old in Thailand, or a twelve-year-old in Cincinnati. I see myself as an awareness raiser. I understand people like me: white, middle-class Americans. We've been blessed by our birthright; how can we not help those who are burdened by theirs?

"Raising awareness means not simply pointing out what is going on over in Thailand or someplace else, but looking at what is happening here in our own lives. This is not only about slavery in foreign factories; it's about how we drive that slavery by insisting on cheaper and cheaper prices for our goods. By our consumerism,

we are the ones who create the demand for slave labor.
This is not only about the horrors of sex slavery but also
about how our participation in the pornography industry
is helping make it profitable.

"Modern-day slavery is a human construction, which
means that we have the ability to do something about it,"
Jeremy says. "God didn't cause slavery, or the poverty
that traps people in slavery, but I would say that God has
a plan for these things *not* to happen: we are that plan.
We are the ones we've been waiting for."

REFLECTION

This eighth beatitude sounds like it has been pieced together from the others, with words about heaven from
the first, justice from the fourth, and persecution from
the ninth beatitude.[2] This is intentional, Scripture scholars
tell us, as it signals the beginning of the end of Jesus' collection of sayings. The ninth beatitude, "Blessed are *you*
persecuted," with its lengthy conclusion that sounds like
a Beethoven coda, marks the end of the collection—but
more about that in the next chapter.[3]

In naming the persecuted as blessed, Matthew sums
up the sayings of Jesus. The persecuted ones are the poor,
the mourning, the meek, the ones hungry and thirsty for
justice, the merciful, the pure in heart, the peacemakers.
God is with them all. As Dietrich Bonhoeffer said about
this beatitude in *The Cost of Discipleship,* those who
work for justice "receive the same promise as the poor,
for in persecution they are their equals in poverty."[4]

The words about persecution express what Matthew's
listeners already knew as a community of Jews following

a way that put them at odds with their tradition. The alternative way of Jesus, honoring the outcast, caring for the least, and upending the status quo—"taking up the cross" and so dying to the way of convention—was dangerous. For Jesus, it led to a Roman cross. For his first followers, and Matthew's community, it meant the pain of ostracism, severing family ties, and leaving behind cherished traditions and comfortable conventions. By the end of the first century, it meant persecution at the hands of Rome. The way of Jesus meant trouble.

As Jeremy says, it's dangerous. Not that Jeremy suffers persecution; he is clear about where the suffering lies. But I would say (I know he wouldn't!) that Jeremy has taken up the cross. For starters, to tell his friends and neighbors and colleagues that we American shoppers are promoting human slavery might not win him a popularity prize or advancement to a coveted pulpit. Jeremy is choosing a dangerous way to see life: from the margins, from the place of the one who is hurting.

This is a choice for a life that takes him away from the economic comfort he once had, a choice to spend his time and his energy for others, a choice for a life that is larger than his own. He has made a choice to practice this beatitude.

Jeremy has made a choice that is something like Peter's choice to drop his fishing nets, as Luke tells it (see Luke 5:1–11).

Peter is just a fisherman, busy with his nets and boats and family obligations. He knows how to count a day's work and a day's pay. He knows the ingredients of the good life for him and his family; not to expect too much or accept too little. But then Jesus comes to Galilee. Peter has heard about this one who upset the folks in Nazareth with that sermon in the synagogue about good news for the poor, release for captives, sight for the blind, liberty for the oppressed. Peter has heard that when Jesus comes around, everything changes. Jesus, with his way of reminding everyone what the prophets said, has a way of threatening the old and promising the new. Jesus even has something to say about fishing: "put out into the deep and let down your nets for a catch" (Luke 5:4 RSV).

The "deeps" are something most of us, including Peter, try to avoid. They are dangerous. Usually sure of himself and his fishing boat, Peter knows that he is up against something new with these words of Jesus—something so new and so powerful that he can't resist. He takes both of his boats out to the deep part of the lake and lets down his nets. And the haul of fish is so big it threatens to rip the nets and sink both of Peter's boats. But that's only the beginning of the story. Out there in the deep, Peter dropped his nets. Back on shore, he drops to his knees and then he drops everything else that is familiar, and he takes to the road with Jesus.

This is dangerous stuff. For Peter and for the rest of us, the encounter with Jesus is dangerous to the way we have lived and the way we might want to live, and it can be dangerous to the way we see ourselves. The encounter with this call to "the deeps" invites us to the blessing of the "kingdom of heaven," as Matthew names it in this beatitude, and it also invites us to see everything in a new way.

First, the encounter lets us see dimensions of ourselves that we might not like. With Peter, who learns on the face of it that he doesn't know everything about fishing, we see that we don't know it all either. With Peter, we are forced to admit we are not what we pretend to be or even what we want to be. With Peter, who says "I am a sinful man," we see the dark corners of our lives come into view. We see the ways we keep ourselves separated from the ones in pain, and we might even see the ways we shut off our own hidden pain. We begin to see the things happening right under our nose—as Jeremy says, on Main Street, USA—that we might not want to see.

But then we can hear the One who says, as he said to Peter, "Do not be afraid." This is the invitation to change, the invitation to that new way of life, a life lived in the presence of God, the kingdom of heaven.

Peter let go of his nets. To practice this beatitude and all the others, we too are invited to let go of what holds us back, the things that catch us up, that keep us stuck, caught in old patterns. We might change our jobs, whether we are catching fish or anything else for a living, or we might change the hold that our jobs have on us. We might stay exactly where we are, doing what we do, but we can choose to give up the defeated feeling that we can't make a difference in the world. And then we can meet the God that is real to us in human flesh, in the small and daily events in our own locale: in that twelve-year-old child ensnared in poverty, in that crazy street lady with the overflowing shopping cart, in that imperfect face in the mirror.

We will find ourselves out in the deeps, and it might just be more surprising than Peter's nets full of fish. When we let go of our proverbial nets and all that holds us back and keeps us comfortable, our world expands, as it did for Peter, and for Jeremy. The things that mattered before don't matter in the same way. We discover new passions, we discover God's passion. In ways large and small—we each need to decide—our personal comfort becomes less important than the common good.

In Luke's Gospel story, Peter sees that his days as a fisherman are over, and his world suddenly becomes even less predictable than a day's catch. He leaves it all and follows. Dangerous.

Peter's story is not a manifesto to leave job and home and family. But it *is* a not-very-subtle illustration that something brand new happens when we choose to follow this Jesus and his beatitudes and his way that led to the cross, something that upsets the expectations of the day and causes us to ask questions like, "What is most important to me in my daily life? Are my nets full? What holds me? What holds me back? What might need to be upset? Who is hurting? How am I connected to that hurt? Where do I see God's presence in our world? What am I doing that keeps me dulled to that presence, that keeps me deaf to that voice?"

Peter drops his fishing nets, leaves his fleet, and joins the Jesus movement. Not everybody is Peter. But everybody is invited to the encounter with God's new way in the world announced in the dangerous man from Nazareth and his alternative way of blessing. Everybody is invited into the deep.

For Further Reflection

1. Jeremy says, "We are the persecutors in ways we never understand, because of our privilege." What do you think he means by this?
2. Can you name a time when you have been asked, like Peter, to "drop your nets" and try something new and unexpected? What was that experience like? What changed for you?

3. What holds you? What holds you back?
4. Where do you see God's presence in our world?
5. What might you do in your local setting to raise awareness about modern-day slavery?
6. In what ways can we support one another in exchanging "personal comfort" for "the common good"? How would you explain the term "the common good"?

CHAPTER NINE

Blessed are you persecuted

"Blessed are you when people revile you and persecute you and utter all kinds of evil against you falsely on my account. Rejoice and be glad, for your reward is great in heaven, for so in the same way they persecuted the prophets who were before you."—Matthew 5:11–12

OBY'S STORY

Obadiah Ballinger bears not only the name of a biblical prophet but also the prophet's vocation: he speaks out, in God's name, for justice.

Unlike his namesake, Oby doesn't thunder on about God's wrath or impending doom. Instead, it is with a quiet tenderness that reveals his own experience of God's love that Oby proclaims God's generous love and wide mercy.

But it wasn't always so.

"I was born and raised in a religious cult," Oby says as the first line of his personal story. "I never learned that God is loving; I was taught that God is stingy with love and abundant with punishment."

Every Friday afternoon throughout Oby's childhood his large family would travel from their southeastern Minnesota farm to the cult compound five hours away in eastern Wisconsin. The weekend was an endless series of lengthy worship services and Bible studies, and Oby remembers the compound of "the brethren" as a place of excessive control where sleep and food deprivation were common practice, along with corporal punishment.

"I thought all churches were like that," he says. "I tried as hard as I could to earn God's love, to earn the cult leaders' love—or at least to be overlooked when it came time for beatings."

When Oby was twelve, his mother divorced his father and left the cult, taking all six children with her. She resumed her abandoned schooling (she'd left college to join the cult) and her plans to become a vet. "She watched over all six of us as a single mother and went to vet school. She's now a practicing veterinarian in Minneapolis," Oby says with obvious pride.

Oby spent his high school years living with his grandparents and attending their Lutheran Church. "I first went to church mostly to hang out, but it quickly became more than that to me," he says. "I still had faith in communities. I had a year of atheism in junior high but I always had a sense that there was a personal dynamic to my faith. I longed for community but I didn't trust it because I'd think 'that's culty.' It took me a while to figure out that community can be genuine."

Oby found a welcoming community in his grandparents' church and became an active member of the youth group. Inspired by his youth pastor, he began to consider a call to ordination. But his place in the church community became problematic.

"By the end of high school I figured out that I was gay and this was a conservative Lutheran church," he said. "I had a very supportive family; my uncle is gay and my grandparents were PFLAG folks.[1] So Grandma was very supportive when I came out. The first thing I told her was:

I don't think I can be a pastor. I'd never heard of a gay pastor. The local church thought it was an abomination; I figured the national church wasn't supportive either. But my Grandma said, 'It's not impossible; you do have the spirit of a minister and you shouldn't give up your dream.'"

In college, on the Sunday after September 11, 2001, Oby found a church that welcomed him. "I was running late that morning and couldn't make it to where I'd planned to go. I stumbled into a UCC church. The minister there prayed for Jews and Muslims, asking that there not be racial profiling in this time of anger. I heard incredible preaching that made sense of the Bible and the gospel and applied it to people's real lives. I didn't know that Christians were so concerned about social justice; all I'd heard before was that you must be saved in a personal salvation sort of way."

Oby was surprised to find that it was not only the Christians in that particular church who were concerned about social justice, but that this was also a central concern of Christianity as a whole. "In college I never met a cause that I didn't like," Oby laughs. "I was always wearing buttons, T-shirts. If I thought that something was a liberal progressive project, I was on board with it, but I didn't know how that connected with the Bible. I thought Christianity stood in the way of social progress and equality. I was a women's studies minor and I was peeved that Christianity was so patriarchal."

Coupling his activism with a religion major, Oby began to discover the roots of the kind of preaching he was hearing in his UCC church. "Shawnthea Monroe, my minister, offered the metaphor of a tree," Oby says. "She told me that the reforms I demanded from my left-leaning branch of the church should be fed through rigorous studies in the trunk and tradition of the faith. If I overlooked the Christian roots for social justice, I would be out on a limb with no support when times grew tough."

Oby went to Yale Divinity School, his minister's alma mater, in search of the grounding he would need "to advocate for change in light of the church's historic gospel profession," as he puts it.

At Yale, Oby deepened his commitment to both social justice activism and what he calls its underpinnings: "I have become concerned about the spiritual sustenance for activism; I'm very concerned about supporting the spirits of those who are on the front lines of social change. I think of myself as an activist-contemplative. To practice this involves a contemplative way of finding God within yourself and in the world, and becoming aware of the promise of God and support of God in the face of life. That's what I try to do with morning devotions, with prayer. I'm reaching out for ground on which to stand as I do the work of advocacy.

"It was this recognition of the need for faith support as we try to make the world a better place that drew me to The Beatitudes Society. First and foremost, our guidance in activism comes from scripture rather than our Enlightenment commitment to individual equal rights."

A new graduate of Yale Divinity School, Oby is now on the front lines himself. He works as the religious organizer for Love Makes a Family, a nonprofit advocacy organization working for equal marriage rights for same-sex couples in Connecticut.[2]

"My role with Love Makes a Family is an educator," Oby says. "I'm educating congregations so they can become advocates for marriage equality. My goal is to build support so that we can pass state legislation approving gay marriage."

For Oby, the core of the message he brings in his work as an organizer and educator is not about legal issues but about the love of God and the need for a new way of seeing.

"My job as a prophet is to manifest God's love," he says. "We believe that God has created us *imago dei,* in the image of God. God has created us for God—to love God back and to love our neighbors as ourselves. I believe the social ills we face are, at bottom, breaches in the relationship between God and human beings and among human beings. We can't see the image of God in the other person and in ourselves."

As one who travels from congregation to congregation speaking on behalf of equality, Oby sees himself as a prophet, but not as one of the persecuted prophets named in the final beatitude.

"I know that there is vitriol spewed about gay people; I've heard it all my life," he says. "But I don't feel that I am persecuted, because I am really caught up in the joy of knowing there's a God who loves me. I hear 're-joice and be glad' when I hear this beatitude. I hear that 'your reward is great' with God, and so I don't hear all the cursing."

But he continues to question the role of the prophet and the nature of discipleship. "I also worry that maybe I am not really risking enough. I worry that I am not really radical enough to be persecuted. I am not really speaking truth to power. How can I risk my neck? How can I do that when I don't want to disrupt my life? Discipleship is really costly, and if your faith life is not costing you something it may well not be true discipleship," he says. "Most of us church people—I include myself—dare to do the possible. We do what's in our sight, what doesn't cost too much, and what we know we can manage. We collect soup cans. We rely on our own strength. But God calls us to step out, to be advocates for those who don't have voices.

"Sometimes I think we need to be more like the prophets of the Bible," Oby says, "to set aside our own self-interest, to set aside our desire for security and stability, to set all that aside to make room for God's disrupting justice."

REFLECTION

I can imagine Jesus leaning forward to speak, almost in a whisper, to make sure they hear this final beatitude: "Blessed are *you, you* my disciples, for all you do on my account." That's just my imagination of course, but this ninth beatitude is different from the previous eight, and Scripture scholars say there's a reason Matthew ended his collection in this way. The switch to direct address, from third to second person, and the extra lengthy conclusion serve to do three things: signal the end of the collection, introduce the rest of the Sermon on the Mount, and also heighten the importance of what is being said.[3] And so what we hear is a note of clear joy in the face of persecution, a promise and a strong invitation to "rejoice and be glad."

Oby, "caught up in the joy of knowing there's a God who loves me," has heard the promise and the invitation in this beatitude. It is a promise of lasting joy with God

(Matthew uses the word *heaven* in deference to the Jewish custom of refraining from naming God)—a joy that begins now and holds for all those who dare, as Oby said, to "make room for God's disrupting justice."

Marriage equality, the kind of justice that Oby seeks in Connecticut, is indeed disruptive, as evidenced by widespread and long-standing church debates about the issue and by recent state ballot initiatives seeking a ban on same-sex marriage. The disruption will be with us for a while yet, but that disruption is to be expected for the followers of Jesus and his unconventional compassion.

Oby's steady commitment to justice and his joyful spirit brings to mind an earlier day of rejoicing. After many long months of parishwide discussion and discernment, my church in Santa Barbara, California, took a step not yet sanctioned by the church or the state. (The story of that discernment is chronicled in Nora Gallagher's book *Practicing Resurrection.*[4])

The day was September 28, 1997, and I was the preacher for the wedding of two long-time members of our church. I don't have a better way to tell the story of that day, or offer a reflection on this beatitude, than simply to offer the sermon here, and to do so in honor of Oby and all who work for a day when everyone has a place at the banquet table:

> We stand today on new ground. It is a new day. We have never been here before and it's a little scary. All beginnings are like that. All weddings. But we all know that today marks a new day not only for Charles and Philip, but a new day for Trinity Episcopal Church, for all of us as a community

of care and support, for all of us who gather to witness this bold step.

Today the church gathers to do what it is uniquely constituted to do: to act not as an agent of the state, but as an agent of grace, as a sign and symbol of God's blessing. We gather as a community directed toward a world marked by the extraordinary vision named in Matthew's Gospel, a world where the poor are lifted up, where the grieving find new life, where the meek come into their own. This world is a world of justice, where the outcasts move from the margins to the center, and the center is changed. Today is about that kind of change. Today marks a step toward that world announced in Matthew's Gospel.

The steps leading to this moment have not been easy ones. As I've talked with you, Charles and Philip, about your journeys, I know that the road to this place has been marked by struggle. I am aware that this day of joy has been preceded by some years of sorrow.

As I've prepared for this day, as I've considered your journey, I've connected with something from my own journey. Let me tell you about another day, in another church. The church is in Durham, England.

On a visit to England several summers ago, my husband Randy and our son and I visited every cathedral we could. Even Ben, ten years old at the time, liked the high gothic arches—he would position himself under the highest arch of the nave and lie back and look straight up—even Ben was impressed with the soaring heights that seemed to reach—and almost achieve—heaven.

We went to Durham not for soaring arches—it is a Norman structure, with heavy, earthbound Romanesque design—we went there on our way to Lindisfarne to see the shrine of St. Cuthbert, the seventh-century monk who had been the prior of the abbey at Lindisfarne. We went there because it is supposed to be a place of healing. The cathedral was built as the final resting place for his bones. Medieval pilgrims traveled from all over Europe to Durham, because St. Cuthbert and his shrine were said to offer miraculous healings.

We entered the cathedral, pulling open the huge heavy door with a huge brass lion's head sanctuary door knocker. I was not ready for what was inside. I was overwhelmed by the power of that interior space. Massive columns of stone carved eight hundred years ago rose up around me. It all felt so strong and sturdy—a mighty fortress indeed. The whole place spoke of power, frankly, the power and might of Norman kings more than the holiness of God.

And then I looked down at the floor. (More than stained glass or high arches, the floors of the cathedrals and abbeys and churches were my favorite. I loved to place my feet on the stones worn concave by centuries of pilgrims and wonder what longings, what hopes, what prayers brought them to these holy places.)

I looked down and saw a long, wide, black marble line inlaid in the stone floor. It stretched across the entire width of the nave, across the back end, the west end. I had never seen anything like it. And then I looked up and saw a framed sign posted on the column, explaining the line. The sign said the marble was laid there, in the 1100s, when the cathedral was built, to keep the women back, to keep the women away from the main part of the church. It was a protective barrier, to keep the altar and St. Cuthbert's holy shrine pure and free from the corrupting influence of women.

As I looked at that black line, another image, another set of lines, came to mind: I remembered diagrams I had seen in a history book of other lines, the holds of slave ships, where African slaves were packed like sardines, lined up row upon row for the voyage to America, kept in place by those lines. Those diagrams, of course, are only relics from the past, long unused, never to be used again. That black line is only a relic from the past, never to be used again.

It hurt to see that line. It hurts to remember it even now, that barrier established in the name of purity. That day, as I stood there, surrounded by the power and might of the church, I thought of the men who had laid that marble and all the women who had stayed behind the line. I thought of the present day Church of England, where the line in the summer of 1992 was still firm against women priests, a line since crossed. We all know about lines.

I made my way the east end, to St. Cuthbert's shrine behind the altar. It was a holy place; simple, stark, marked by the prayers of centuries. It felt like a place of healing. I prayed there for healing, for an end to the lines we build, for the lines in the church, for the lines in my own heart, for the barriers I keep in place, for the people I keep on the other side of my barriers.

That line on the floor of Durham Cathedral serves no purpose anymore. It is a relic from the past.

I believe that the day that marble was laid, God wept. And I believe that every time we cross a line like that, God dances.

Today, we cross the line. Today, old barriers lose their power, old wounds can lose their sting. Today, as we gather our collective courage and our good will, healing is possible because we gather to celebrate something larger than ourselves. Today we celebrate not only the love of these two men but also the love of a God who invites all of us to cross the line, to stay back no longer, to step into healing and into hope and into joy.

Today, we cross that line. And so today, God is dancing. Amen.

For Further Reflection

1. Oby's grandmother was a significant support in his early years. Can you describe someone like that in your past and how she or he supported you?
2. Oby grew up not realizing that "Christians were so concerned about social justice; all I'd heard before

was that you must be saved in a personal salvation sort of way." Describe your own journey in understanding your church's teaching about social justice and personal salvation.

3. Oby believes that the social ills we face result from being unable "to see the image of God in the other person and in ourselves." What makes it possible to recognize the image of God in someone or in ourselves?

4. Oby describes himself as an "activist-contemplative," with a daily prayer practice that supports his advocacy work. Can you name some practices that give you "ground on which to stand"? In your life, what is the relationship between action and contemplation?

5. Can you describe any "lines" you have encountered in your life? Are the lines still in place? What would it take to cross them?

CHAPTER TEN

Being salt and light

"You are the salt of the earth; but if salt has lost its
taste, how can its saltiness be restored? It is no longer
good for anything, but is thrown out and trampled
underfoot. You are the light of the world. A city built
on a hill cannot be hid. No one after lighting a lamp
puts it under the bushel basket, but on the lampstand,
and it gives light to all in the house. In the same way,
let your light shine before others, so that they may
see your good works and give glory to your Father in
heaven."—Matthew 5:13–17

Rejoice, be glad, and get to work: be salt and light,
and let your light shine. Matthew ends his collection of
Jesus' wisdom sayings on a high note, with a promise
of rejoicing with God. And then he adds a few lines of
instruction to the invitation, words that serve as a bridge
to the rest of the Sermon on the Mount: "You are the
salt of the earth, you are the light of the world . . . let
your light shine."

Jesus' first listeners knew that salt was necessary for
life, a notion reinforced by the many references in the Hebrew Scriptures to salt's essential nature. Thus the prophet
Elisha sprinkled salt into the spring at Jericho to purify
the water (2 Kings 2:21). To eat salt with another person
was a sign of loyalty, sort of a passing of the peace pipe,
a breaking of bread, a sign of commonality (Num. 18:19.)
Priests strew salt on sacrifices and seasoned incense with

salt. Parents rubbed salt all over their newborn baby's body as protection against all kinds of ills (Ezek. 16:4).

Salt is basic. When I was a child and heard my parents say that someone was "the salt of the earth," I knew they were giving the ultimate compliment: that these were solid citizens; loyal, trustworthy, brave, God-fearing people (and probably Scandinavian Lutherans too!). Salt was something we understood. And when I heard the words about "salt of the earth" in Sunday school, I knew it was nothing exotic like the other things that turned up in the Bible; this was not frankincense or myrrh, this was plain old table salt, the round blue box sitting on the back of the kitchen stove. Salt was regular, not fancy; salt was for every day, not just company. If we were to be like salt, it meant we were to be useful.

But salt doesn't work alone. It preserves, it adds flavor, it zests things up. It changes the soil, the water, the function of the human body. For salt to work, it must be used *with* something. To be a disciple, Jesus is saying, is to be like salt, mixed right into the middle of life, adding some zest and making a difference.

And light is like salt. It illumines; it brings other things to life. Like salt, light is essential for life and growth. It illumines things and brings the hidden into view. Light is measured by what it does, by how it changes its environs.

In these words about salt and light, Jesus is telling his disciples that they must be effective. They must change their surroundings.

Glen Stassen says that this expression about salt is intended to praise the distinctive witness of the ascetic Qumran community of Jesus' day who lived by the Dead

Sea and made table salt by evaporating the salty waters
of that sea. "They were indeed a right salty community,"
he writes. "They were definitely different from the world
and its compromises."[1]

We, too, are to be "different from the world." Indeed, the beatitudes are a description of a way of living
quite distinct from the prevailing practices of economic
and political injustice. But being different is not enough.
Jesus praises the Essenes at Qumran, but also adds a bit
of a dig: that difference must be seen; that light cannot
be hidden "under a bushel" where none can see it. The
problem with the Qumran community, Stassen says, was
that they kept themselves hidden down by the Dead Sea,
living in retreat from the world. The followers of Jesus
cannot be separatists; they must be the ones who show
up in the dark places of the world and light it up with
the compassion of God. As Stefani knows, we are the
ones called to expand the church beyond stained glass
and stone walls.

"Unless we are walking the talk, we are not authentic
salt; we are no different from the sand underfoot, nor are
we a light that actually shines in the world. If we are not
doing justice for Jesus' sake, the world has no reason to
heed us, to allow us to disturb them," says Stassen.[2]

To live the beatitudes is to be the people who "disturb"
the world. As Stassen says, "The way people see God's
light is not because we sing praise songs but because of
our actions."[3] We are to be, as Mary Emily would say, the
ones who "cause trouble, trouble for transformation."

This salt business, this light image, can sound like the
ingredients of a theology that says "prove yourself." Work
hard at it, or you might not make it. This is the theology

that makes the beatitudes "entrance requirements" to a kind of heaven reached by achievement and based on reward and punishment.

Being salt and light, letting that light shine, *is* hard work. Living the beatitudes *does* mean hard work. It means hard work like Kent's steadfast commitment to just peacemaking, finding alternative solutions to violence and excessive consumption. It means Greta building those bridges she won't cross and April imagining a church that teaches transformative love. Living the beatitudes means the hard work of social change, challenging the economic and social structures of oppression, exclusion, and domination. Being salt and light means mixing it up with the public and political issues of the day—not staying safely hidden doing good deeds only within our church communities—but stepping out to push for what Oby calls "God's disturbing justice."

This kind of pushing against the status quo can be dangerous, as Jeremy knows. But for us the real danger here is that we can misinterpret the beatitudes—and indeed the Christian life—as a set of high ideals reached by our own merit and struggle. We can hear the beatitudes as an exhortation to grit our teeth and put our shoulders to the wheel, and start calculating whether we are pushing hard enough. We can forget that blessing comes *not* as reward for our good work, but simply because we are joining the ongoing liberating presence and work of God in the world. We can forget who we are, and so "lose our taste."

Jesus is saying that we are already salty, light-filled people, that we already have within us the very elements of earth and heaven, equipped to be God's partners in compassionately caring for the creation. We are invited to be nothing more and nothing less than who God created us to be. We are invited, as Alex might say, to remember whose we are.

The beatitudes, as Stassen says, "do not promise distant well-being and success; they celebrate the reality that God is already acting to deliver us." Stassen says.[4] Grace is already in our midst; we have seen it in Jesus and his "politics of compassion."

So the beatitudes are invitation rather than exhortation. As both invitation and gift, they offer the way for us to participate in God's abundance, as Chris says, to be part of the transforming Spirit of God working for growth and change. Accepting the beatitudes—indeed, all of our lives—as gift keeps us from the seduction of our own effort and makes room for grace.

In the words of ethicist Timothy Sedgwick, "Gift expresses the experience of grace that stands at the heart of creation. . . . We can either accept or reject this gift. We thereby either withdraw from the world . . . or else we engage the world . . . we either atrophy or grow, contract or enlarge as we either accept or reject the gift of life. To accept is to give thanks and to care for our world."[5]

I learned something about this invitation and gift in a cemetery. Several years ago, my family and I traveled to Norway to trace family roots. We visited lots of cemeteries, looking for tombstones with family names on them. This is a daunting task: my ancestors bear the names of Ole or Lars or Anders or Halvor, and the cemeteries were filled with row upon row of names like Ole Olson or Lars Olson or Anders Larson or Lars Anderson. We wandered for hours searching for the right Ole or Anders, and in the process found that the stories on the tombstones became more fascinating than the names. The cemeteries in Norway are libraries of stone tablets, filled with granite stories of the village and its traditions. In a few terse lines, the essence of each person and their place in the local culture is revealed. Here lies the sturdy farmer, here the brave fisherman, here the loving mother, the faithful pastor, the revered village teacher. Only a few words for each stone story, only the most important.

And then we found a tombstone with a very short story, just one word: *Takk*. Thanks. That Norwegian ended life with that single word to sum it all up. Thanks. Imagine that. Imagine the summation of your life as "thanks."

That single word on that tombstone is the story of a life lived in awareness of God's grace: a life lived in thanksgiving for the learning that comes in hard times and the surprising joy of good times, a life lived in awareness of God's enlivening presence in all times.

If I had to write one word on my tombstone, I'd like it to be *Takk*. I'd like to be able to say thanks for all that life has offered me, all the abundance, for long years of deep joy and full days of hard work. But, God willing, I'm not ready for a tombstone for a long time yet. And so my way of saying thanks to God for all the grace and gift of life is to practice the beatitudes, mindful that I practice not ever to "get it right," but to keep saying "yes, thanks" to God's invitation to participate in "causing trouble for transformation," and to celebrate the reality that God is already liberating us to join in the work of growth and change. And the best part of practicing these beatitudes is that we can only do this together; it takes all of us, the whole community, Chris and Stefani and Alex and Greta and April and Mary Emily and Kent and Jeremy and Oby and all the others, the beloved community gathered around God's table of abundance, where there is always room for one more. I can imagine this table. Maybe the meal is Mary Emily's pot of soup. And I can imagine a way we might give thanks. It's a prayer of hospitality and celebration, a blessing from the Celtic tradition known as St. Brigid's prayer.[6] This is a beatitudes prayer that says "rejoice and be glad":

> I should like a great lake of beer for the King of
>   Kings.
> I should like the angels of Heaven to be drinking it
>   through time eternal.
> I should like excellent meats of belief and pure
>   piety.
> I should like the men of Heaven at my house.
> I should like barrels of peace at their disposal.
> I should like for them cellars of mercy.
> I should like cheerfulness to be their drinking.
> I should like Jesus to be there among them.
> I should like the three Marys of illustrious renown
>   to be with us.
> I should like the people of Heaven, the poor, to be
>   gathered around from all parts.

FOR FURTHER REFLECTION

1. Describe someone in your life who is "the salt of the earth."

2. Is there a place nearby where your church might "expand beyond the stained glass" to shine God's light?

3. What kind of "pushing up against the status quo" do you think is needed right now in your community or in your country?

4. Try to describe your experience of "the learning that comes in hard times" or "the surprising joy of good times."

5. If you could choose words to put on your tombstone, what might they be?

Thanksgiving

Most mornings, I pray the rosary, an Anglican rosary of blue and gold beads made by a child in our church school. As my fingers round the small set of beads, I begin with thanksgivings, naming the names of many people, and I end by praying the beatitudes, one bead for each. The names that follow are on those beads and in my heart.

So many people made this book possible. Each name is a another story that has shaped my life and ministry and writing, but I will be brief in these few lines. I am thankful for each and every one:

First, thanks to Michael and Frances Hall Kieschnick, founders of The Beatitudes Society, for their bold vision, generous spirits, and commitment to the next generation of leaders. I am particularly grateful for Michael's incisive questions impelling us forward to the next challenge, and Frannie's gracious and buoyant hospitality providing us all with strength for the journey.

Thanks to the students and alums of The Beatitudes Society, each of the nine who shared their stories and shaped this book, and all the other student, faculty and professional members of The Beatitudes Society: the Summer Fellows, the Campus Chapter Conveners, the online bloggers and the Gulf Coast builders, all the "BeAts" who participate in workshops and service learning projects and reflection-action groups, and are working to articulate a Christianity that speaks for the voiceless. These emerging leaders are turning the world upside down, in the spirit of Jesus, and each person I meet gives me hope.

Thanks to the Friends of The Beatitudes Society, who support these emerging leaders with generous gifts of time and treasure, and to our Board of Advisors, who support our mission in so many creative ways, and gave me the time to do the writing.

Thanks to the "small but mighty" staff of The Beatitudes Society, Stephanie Wert Borrett and Betty Segui Wenzel, for their skills and creativity and commitment to the students. And thanks to our Junior Office Worker, Grace Wenzel, for huge measures of joy and grace.

Thanks to Alex Carpenter, who brainstormed the idea of illustrating the beatitudes through the lives of the students, and who wanted to call this book "Shakin' the Beatitudes."

Thanks to Marcus Borg, for his abundant gifts of time and consultation over the years; I am honored to have his foreword on this book.

Thanks to Fred Borsch for years of friendship, for continuing commitment to students as a faculty advisor for our chapter at the Lutheran Theological School at Philadelphia, and for consultation on this book.

Thanks to Glen Stassen for consultation about the beatitudes and the Sermon on the Mount, and commitment as faculty advisor to our chapter at Fuller Seminary.

Thanks to Diana Butler Bass, who welcomed all my "first-time author" questions with grace and skill, and is always inspiring and encouraging all of us to practice a Christianity of courage and compassion.

Thanks to Nora Gallagher, who encouraged me at just the right moments, and has always told me the truth with love and grace.

Thanks to Barbara Brown Taylor, who taught me the difference between gift and skill, and gave me courage to accept a gift with thanks.

Thanks to John O'Neil, who gave me gifts of time and wise counsel at the very start.

Thanks to David Schlafer, for unfailing encouragement and his preacher's ear and eye for a good word.

Thanks to Mark Asman, priest and friend, and to all the people of Trinity Episcopal in Santa Barbara for sharing their stories and their lives with me; for listening with the ears of their hearts to some of the stories included here; and for honoring me with the title of Preacher-in-Residence.

Thanks to Rabbi Leonard Beerman, Dr. George Regas, and Dr. William Rankin, for showing me that that people of faith must always engage the issues of the day and the needs of the world, as we take up the holy work of *tikkun olam*, repairing the world.

Thanks to Jane Olson, for showing me that loving care for the world and each other is not limited by geographical boundaries or linear time.

Thanks to Richard Bass and the team at Alban for guidance and enthusiasm for this project.

Thanks to Ulrike Guthrie, whose fine editing made this project a great joy as we traded manuscripts across the time zones. She has a keen ear for just-the-right-word and a theologian's discernment for the heart of the matter. Her unfailing kindness and encouragement made all the difference to this first-time author.

Thanks to Bethany Thornton, for always being at the ready as friend, fellow writer, and "first reader."

Thanks to Mary Richardson, "best-friend-since-childhood," who shared bike rides to the library, good books on the front porch, and good talks ever since, about this book and everything else.

Thanks to my parents, Jean and Cully Sutherland, first source of abundant blessing, who taught me in their living and in their dying that the most important words are "I love you" and "thank you."

And last in this list but first in my heart: thanks to my husband Randy, for abiding adventure, and for always showing me that "in returning and rest we shall be saved, in quietness and confidence shall be our strength;" and to our son Benjamin, for being my best and toughest critic, and for carrying the fire. Takk for alt.

Notes

Epigraph

1. I use the English translation "justice" rather than "righteousness" for the fourth and eighth beatitudes, following my reading of both Marcus Borg in his *Jesus: Uncovering the Life, Teachings, and Relevance of a Religious Revolutionary* (San Francisco: HarperOne, 2006), 190, and Glen Stassen in his *Living the Sermon on the Mount: A Practical Hope for Grace and Deliverance* (San Francisco: Jossey-Bass, 2006), 32–37 and 51–53.

Introduction: Parables for a new generation

1. The Beatitudes Society develops and sustains a national network of progressive Christian leaders in seminaries and divinity schools who advocate for justice, compassion, and peace.
2. Stassen, *Living the Sermon on the Mount*, 41.
3. Borg, *Jesus*, 260.

Chapter One: Blessed are the poor in spirit

1. Stassen, *Living the Sermon on the Mount*, 4.
2. "God commends this" is a quotation from Marcus Borg (personal conversation). The idea of the beatitudes as God's invitation to change our world, or beatitudes as transforming initiatives, is the thesis of Stassen's *Living the Sermon on the Mount*.
3. Robert A. Guelich, *The Sermon on the Mount: A Foundation for Understanding* (Waco, TX: Word Books, 1982), 70–72.

4. Stassen, *Living the Sermon on the Mount*, 18.
5. See Stassen, *Living the Sermon on the Mount*, 24–37, for his thorough treatment of the characteristics of the reign of God.
6. See Borg, *Jesus*, 186–190, for a rich explanation of the new kingdom announced by Jesus.
7. Leonardo Boff and Clodovis Boff, *Introducing Liberation Theology* (Maryknoll, NY: 1987), 43–44.
8. Daniel Hartnett, "Remembering the Poor: An Interview with Gustavo Gutierrez," *America*, Feb. 3, 2003.
9. Tracy Kidder, *Mountains Beyond Mountains: The Quest of Dr. Paul Farmer, a Man Who Would Cure the World* (New York: Random House, 2004).

Chapter Two: Blessed are those who mourn

1. See Mark 5:21–43, Luke 8:40–56; Matthew 9:18–26.
2. Letty M. Russell, *The Future of Partnership* (Philadelphia: Westminster, 1979).

Chapter Three: Blessed are the meek

1. Clarence Jordan, *Sermon on the Mount* (Valley Forge, PA: Judson Press, 1952), 12.
2. Joan Chittister, *The Rule of Benedict: Insight for the Ages* (New York: Crossroad, 1995), 62.
3. Ibid.
4. Ibid., 74.
5. Sallie McFague, *Life Abundant: Rethinking Theology and Economy for a Planet in Peril* (Minneapolis: Augsburg Fortress, 2001), 36.
6. Ibid., 14.
7. Ibid., 140.
8. Ibid., 122.
9. Ibid.

Chapter Four: Blessed are those who hunger and
  thirst for justice

1. www.flobots.com.
2. As noted above, I use the English translation "justice" rather than "righteousness" for the fourth and eight beatitudes, following my reading of Borg in *Jesus* and Stassen in *Living the Sermon on the Mount*.
3. Stassen, *Living the Sermon on the Mount*, 52.
4. Borg, *Jesus*, 185.

Chapter Five: Blessed are the merciful

1. Dennis Hamm, *The Beatitudes in Context* (Wilmington, DE: Michael Glazier, 1990), 96.
2. Frederick H. Borsch, *Many Things in Parables: Extravagent Stories of New Community* (Philadelphia: Fortress, 1988), 66.

Chapter Six: Blessed are the pure in heart

1. Dale C. Allison, *The Sermon on the Mount: Inspiring the Moral Imagination* (New York: Crossroad Publishing Co., 1999), 51.
2. Stassen, *Living the Sermon on the Mount,* 56
3. Allison, *The Sermon on the Mount,* 51.
4. Marcus Borg, *Meeting Jesus Again for the First Time: The Historical Jesus and the Heart of Christian Faith* (San Francisco: HarperSanFrancisco, 1994), 58. The entire third chapter of this pithy book presents a full discussion of Jesus's politics of compassion.

Chapter Seven: Blessed are the peacemakers

1. Community Supported Agriculture farms offer produce subscriptions, with which buyers receive a weekly or monthly basket of produce, flowers, fruits, eggs,

milk, coffee, or other farm products. "A CSA (for Community Supported Agriculture) is a way for the food buying public to create a relationship with a farm and to receive a weekly basket of produce. By making a financial commitment to a farm, people become 'members' (or 'shareholders,' or 'subscribers') of the CSA. Most CSA farmers prefer that members pay for the season up front, but some farmers will accept weekly or monthly payments. Some CSAs also require that members work a small number of hours on the farm during the growing season." See www.localharvest.org/csa/.

2. The Interfaith Center to Reverse the Arms Race is based in Pasadena, California.

3. Rabbi Leonard Beerman, Leo Baeck Temple, Los Angeles, was cofounder with The Rev. Dr. George Regas of the Interfaith Center to Reverse the Arms Race.

4. Dwight Eisenhower, speech to American Society of Newspaper Editors, 1953.

5. Glen Stassen, *Just Peacemaking: Transforming Initiatives for Justice and Peace* (Louisville, KY: Westminster John Knox, 1992).

6. Stassen, *Living the Sermon on the Mount*, 65.

7. Ibid., 68.

8. Ibid., 98–100.

9. Glen Stassen, ed., *Just Peacemaking: Ten Practices for Abolishing War* (Cleveland: Pilgrim Press, 2004), 11.

10. The Ten Initiatives: (1) Support nonviolent direct action. (2) Take independent initiatives to reduce threat. (3) Use cooperative conflict resolution. (4) Acknowledge responsibility for conflict and injustice and seek repentance and forgiveness. (5) Advance democracy, human rights, and religious liberty. (6) Foster just and sustainable economic development. (7) Work with emerging

cooperative forces in the international system. (8) Strengthen the United Nations and international efforts for cooperation and human rights. (9) Reduce offensive weapons and weapons trade. (10) Encourage grassroots peacemaking groups and voluntary associations.

11. Desmond Tutu, *No Future without Forgiveness*, Double-day, 1999, p.30.
12. Ibid., 31.

Chapter Eight: Blessed are those who are persecuted
  for justice

1. Jon Sobrino, *The Principle of Mercy: Taking the Cru-cified People from the Cross* (Maryknoll, NY: Orbis, 1994), 54.
2. As noted above, I use the English translation "justice" rather than "righteousness" for the fourth and eight beatitudes, following my reading of Borg in *Jesus* and Stassen in *Living the Sermon on the Mount*.
3. Allison, *The Sermon on the Mount*, 55–56.
4. Dietrich Bonhoeffer, *The Cost of Discipleship* (New York, Macmillan, 1963), 127.

Chapter Nine: Blessed are you persecuted

1. Parents, Families and Friends of Lesbians and Gays (www.pflag.org).
2. Love Makes a Family (www.lmfct.org).
3. Allison, *The Sermon on the Mount*, 56.
4. Nora Gallagher, *Practicing Resurrection: A Memoir of Work, Doubt, Discernment, and Moments of Grace* (New York: Knopf, 2004).

Chapter Ten: Being salt and light

1. Stassen, *The Sermon on the Mount*, 60.
2. Ibid., 61.

3. Ibid.

4. Ibid., 41.

5. Timothy Sedgwick, *Sacramental Ethics: Paschal Identity and the Christian Life* (Philadelphia: Fortress, 1987), 65.

6. Several versions of St. Brigid's prayer are available. I found this one on the website for St. Brigid's Parish in Westbury, New York: www.saintbrigid.net.